ADDICTIVE
THINKING *and*

THE ADDICTIVE
PERSONALITY

Two Books in One
Includes:

ADDICTIVE THINKING
Second Edition

BY ABRAHAM J. TWERSKI, M.D.
with a foreword by John Wallace, Ph.D., CAC

THE ADDICTIVE PERSONALITY
Second Edition

BY CRAIG NAKKEN
with a foreword by Damian McElrath, Ph.D.

MJF BOOKS
NEW YORK

Editor's Note: Hazelden offers a variety of information on chemical dependency and related areas. Our publications do not necessarily represent Hazelden's programs, nor do they officially speak for any Twelve Step organization.

Published by MJF Books
Fine Communications
322 Eighth Avenue
New York, NY 10001

Addictive Thinking and The Addictive Personality
Library of Congress Catalog Card Number 99-70057
ISBN 1-56731-331-0

QM   14   13   12   11   10   9   8

THE ADDICTIVE PERSONALITY

Second Edition

CRAIG NAKKEN

with a foreword by Damian McElrath, Ph.D.

*To my wife, Jane, and to Nature,
both of whom have taught me
much about myself, relationships,
beauty, and love.*

Contents

Foreword

First published in February 1988, *The Addictive Personality* has reached a wide audience. It is not difficult to uncover the reason for the popularity of this work. Addiction is a very powerful affliction, and this compact volume, written in an attractive style and comprehensive manner, provides a very powerful and poignant description of the process, its stages and consequences. The unanimous testimony and verdict of recovering people is that *The Addictive Personality* portrays an eerie *déjà vu* picture of their personal struggle with their addictive selves, the destruction of their relationships, the resulting experience of terrible isolation, and their descent into despair and hopelessness. The book serves as an exposé of the lives of all addicts who have moved from the "land of the living" to the surreal land of objects.

Nakken's description of the three stages of the addictive process leading to the emergence of the addictive personality resonates with the experiences of those who have been ensnared by this "cunning, baffling, and powerful" illness.

Nakken's knowledge and experience in dealing with the victims of addiction over the years sets the book apart from dry scientific analyses of addiction and pop explanations that promise magical elixirs from an illness that is often too easily diagnosed.

I am honored to have been asked to write the foreword to this second edition. I have a great affection for Nakken as a friend of many years and a warm reverence for his book, which has proven a valuable source of knowledge and wisdom for myself and the audiences before whom I have lectured over the past decade on the topic of chemical dependency.

What is particularly significant about this work is that the process of addiction and recovery can be viewed as the penultimate paradigm of the core of spirituality—it represents what spirituality is all about. The dying-rising metaphor played out in the drama of the struggle between the addictive and real selves is at the heart of meaningful spirituality. In that real struggle the author has caught and depicted what has been one of the most important and enduring themes in the history of Western thought—the dialectic between the two selves. Recovering addicts and their spiritual journeys can tell and teach us much.

Damian McElrath, Ph.D.

Introduction

This book is written to help its readers better understand the process of addiction and the development of an addictive personality. It seeks to broaden people's minds about the depth and dimensions of one of the most widespread and costly illnesses facing us today. It is my intention to give the reader a better idea of addiction, understanding what people become addicted to and what happens inside the people who suffer from this illness.

The term *addiction* has moved from having a very limited focus—being associated almost entirely with alcohol and other drugs—to a much broader definition. There are millions of addicts who have never used mood-altering chemicals in their rituals of getting high. Food addicts, addictive gamblers, sex addicts, shoplifters, workaholics, addictive spenders, and many others live lives of emotional isolation, shame, and despair caused by their own brands of addiction. This book is dedicated to those who struggle to have their suffering understood and their addictions recognized. It is also written to help recovering addicts better monitor their identified addictions and prevent their transformation into other addictions.

PART *1*

Addiction as a Process

Over the years, addiction has been described in many different ways—a moral weakness, a lack of willpower, an inability to face the world, a physical sickness, and a spiritual illness. If you are a family member or a friend of a practicing addict, you may have more colorful ways of describing addiction. However, addiction can be more accurately described and defined in the following way:

Nearly all human beings have a deep desire to feel happy and to find peace of mind and soul. At times in our lives, most of us find this wholeness of peace and beauty, but then it slips away, only to return at another time. When it leaves us, we feel sadness and even a slight sense of mourning. This is one of the natural cycles of life, and it's not a cycle we can control.

To some extent, we can help these cycles along, but for the most part they're uncontrollable—all of us must go through them. We can either accept these cycles and learn from them or fight them, searching instead for elusive happiness.

Addiction can be viewed as an attempt to control these uncontrollable cycles. When addicts use a particular object, such as a substance or an event to produce a desired mood change, they believe they can control these cycles, and at first they can. Addiction, on its most basic level, is an attempt to control and fulfill this desire for happiness.

Addiction must be viewed as a process that is progressive. Addiction must be seen as an illness that undergoes continuous development from a definite, though often unclear, beginning toward an end point.

We can draw a strong comparison between addiction and cancer. For us to understand all the different forms of cancer, we must first understand what they all have in common. All cancers share a similar process: the uncontrolled multiplying of cells. Similarly, we must first understand what all addictions and addictive processes have in common: the out-of-control and aimless searching for wholeness, happiness, and peace through a relationship with an object or event. No matter what the addiction is, every addict engages in a relationship with an object or event in order to produce a desired mood change, state of intoxication, or trance state.

- The alcoholic experiences a mood change while drinking at the neighborhood bar.
- The food addict experiences a mood change by bingeing or starving.
- The addictive gambler experiences a mood change by placing bets on football games and then watching the action on television.
- The shoplifter experiences a mood change when stealing clothing from a department store.
- The sex addict experiences a mood change while browsing in a pornographic bookstore.
- The addictive spender experiences a mood change by going on a shopping spree.
- The workaholic experiences a mood change by staying at work to accomplish another task even though he or she is needed at home.

Although all of the objects or events described are vastly different, they all produce desired mood changes in the addicts who engage in them.

Types of Highs

Addicts are attracted to certain types of mood changes or highs. Harvey Milkman and Stanley Sunderwirth, in *Craving for Ecstasy: The Consciousness & Chemistry of Escape,* speak of different but specific addictive highs to which people are attracted: arousal, satiation, and fantasy. Arousal and satiation are the most common, followed by fantasy, which is part of all addictions.

Both arousal and satiation are attractive, cunning, baffling, and powerful highs. Arousal comes from amphetamines, cocaine, ecstasy, and the first few drinks of alcohol, and from the behaviors of gambling, sexual acting out, spending, stealing, and so on. Arousal causes sensations of intense, raw, unchecked power and gives feelings of being untouchable and all-powerful. It speaks directly to the drive for power. (This is described more fully in the recovery section, starting on page 65.) Arousal makes addicts believe they can achieve happiness, safety, and fulfillment. Arousal gives the addict the feeling of omnipotence while it subtly drains away all power. To get more power, addicts return to the object or event that provides the arousal and eventually become dependent on it. Arousal addicts become swamped by fear: they fear their loss of power and they fear others will discover how powerless they truly are.

Unlike the power trip of an arousal high, a satiation high gives the addict a feeling of being full, complete, and beyond pain. (Arousal gives the addict the feeling that the pain can be defeated.) Heroin, alcohol, marijuana, Valium, and various behaviors such as overeating, watching TV, or playing slot machines all produce satiation highs.

The satiation high is attractive to certain types of addicts because it numbs the sensations of pain or distress. This pain-free state lasts as long as the individual remains in the mood change created by the addictive ritual. But this type of high attaches the unknowing addict to the grief process. The trance always fades away and sensations always disappear, leaving the addict with the original pain plus the loss of the pleasurable sensations. Over time, satiation addicts are forced to act out more often (if they're behavioral addicts) or increase their dosages (if they're substance abusers). The satiation high gains control over the person, always promising relief from pain. Ultimately, however, the pain returns, deeper and more persistent, until it turns into grief and despair.

Trance

It is helpful to view intoxication—the mood change of the addictive ritual—as a trance state, especially when examining behavioral addictions such as gambling, spending, and sexual acting out.

The trance state is a state of detachment, a state of separation from one's physical surroundings. In the trance, one can live in two worlds simultaneously, floating back and forth between the addictive world and the real world, often without others suspecting it.

The trance allows addicts to detach from the pain, guilt, and shame they feel, making it extremely attractive. The addict becomes increasingly skillful at living in the trance and using it to cover painful feelings. In the process, he or she gets a sense of power and control, but also becomes dependent on the trance, which is part of the progression of the addictive process.

The addict views the trance state as a solution to a problem. "Gambling allowed me to be with people without really being with them," said one compulsive gambler, whose acting out became uncontrollable after her husband died. The trance salved her grief and sorrow. It filled up her emptiness. She felt no pain as long as she was in the casino. Addiction and the trance offered her a solution, and she used it as long as her savings and insurance monies held out. Then she was forced to confront the reality of her losses, and the blow was even more devastating. Not only had she lost her husband but also the money they had put aside to support her. Addiction takes and takes, and then takes some more.

Our attraction to trance-like sensations grows out of our natural desire for transcendence to contact and live within spiritual principles. It is our desire to reconnect with the divine. The sensations of the trance produce a feeling in the individual that connection has taken place. It creates a virtual reality in which the spiritual experience seems real, but is in fact only illusionary. True spiritual experiences give us increased meaning and the skills to connect with meaning again, with healing and compassion. They give us a stronger belief in relationships and humanity. After experiencing the quasi-spiritual experience of the addictive trance, people are left with the pain and anxiety they were trying to escape, in addition to the emptiness created when the soul realizes that no true connection has taken place.

Thus, the trance state is a part of the definition of addiction as a spiritual illness. Addiction is an illness in which people believe in and seek spiritual connection through objects and behaviors that can only produce temporary sensations. These repeated, vain attempts to connect with the Divine produce hopelessness, fear, and grieving that further alienate the addict from spirituality and humanity.

Extending the Addiction Field

Addiction has been viewed in a very limited way, mainly because the treatment of addiction is a relatively young field. Addiction treatment on any sizable scale began with

Alcoholics Anonymous in 1935, which concerned itself with alcoholism, a specific form of addiction. In addition, while most fields of study start with a general knowledge of a subject that gradually becomes more specific, our knowledge about addiction started with a specific form of addiction that gradually has been broadened to help people with many types of addiction. Moreover, the addiction treatment field was not started by a group of professionals, but by people who suffered from one specific form of addiction. As more about the nature of addiction was learned from these pioneers, it was found that their principles of recovery could also help people with other addictions. Thus came the start of Gamblers Anonymous, Narcotics Anonymous, Overeaters Anonymous, Sex Addicts Anonymous, Shoplifters Anonymous, Spenders Anonymous, and other Twelve Step self-help groups.

Why do certain principles of recovery work so effectively for all of these different groups? The apparent reason is that the same illness, addiction, is being treated. We are starting to see that there are many forms of addiction; though they are different, they have core similarities. In the following pages, we will examine these similarities.

Acting Out

Acting out—a term that will be used frequently throughout this book—takes place when an addict engages in addictive behaviors or addictive mental obsessions. Here are some examples:

- Sex addicts cruising sections of town where they are most likely to find prostitutes.
- Compulsive gamblers studying racing forms.
- Compulsive eaters going to different stores to buy food, fearing clerks will recognize and think badly of them.
- Addictive spenders making purchases.

For the addict, acting out is a way to create certain feelings that cause the emotional and mental shift that the addict desires. By acting out, either through thoughts or behavior, the addict learns to create feelings of being relaxed, excited, or in control. The addict can also create feelings of fear, self-disgust, shame, and self-hate. Most of all, the addict achieves an illusion of being in control through acting out.

Addiction becomes an attempt to make emotional sense out of life. Addicts believe on an emotional level that they are being fulfilled. The trance created by the acting out is often described by addicts as a time in which they feel alive and complete. This is especially true in the earlier stages of the addiction process.

Nurturing through Avoidance

Addiction and the mood change created by acting out is a very seductive process in which the addict is emotionally seduced into believing that he or she can be nurtured by objects or events.

We can get temporary relief from objects and events, but we can't get real nurturing from them. All of us have issues, pains, frustrations, and memories we would rather not have to face. At times, we have all used objects or events to avoid facing these. Addiction, however, becomes a lifestyle in which the person loses control of the use of objects and events and gets locked into an emotional evading of life. Addicts keep delaying life issues as a way of nurturing themselves.

All of us have the potential to form addictive relationships with a number of different objects or events, especially during stressful times when we would welcome a promise of relief and comfort. However, avoiding reality and responsibility by the addictive use of objects and events is an ineffective way of self-nurturing. The mood change created by acting out creates only an illusion of being nurtured. For example, the food addict binges after a fight with his partner and finds the illusion of peace. For the moment, he feels full both physically and emotionally instead of empty. During such moments, there is an intense sense of comfort. In a similar way, the compulsive gambler gets lost in the action and feels excited, confident, and sure of herself. This time she knows she has picked a winner.

Slowly, addicts start to depend on the addictive process for a sense of nurturing and definition of who they are. Their lives become the pursuit of their addiction.

Emotional Logic

Addiction starts out as an emotional illusion that is entrenched in the addict before others around the addict or even the addict himself realizes that an addictive relationship has been formed. The addict starts to build a defense system to protect the addictive belief system against attacks from others, but only after the addiction is well established on an emotional level. On a thinking, intellectual level, the addict knows that an object cannot bring emotional fulfillment. Alcoholics have heard the old saying "You can't escape into a bottle." Workaholics know "there's more to life than just work." Addictive spenders understand "money can't buy happiness."

The illness of addiction begins very deep within a person, and his or her suffering takes place on an emotional level. Intimacy, positive or negative, is an emotional experience that is not logically evaluated. Addiction is an emotional relationship with an object or event, through which addicts try to meet their needs for intimacy. When looked at in this way, the logic of addiction starts to become clear. When compulsive eaters feel sad, they eat to feel better. When alcoholics start to feel out of control with anger, they have a couple of drinks to get back in control.

Addiction is very logical and follows a logical progression, but this progression is totally based on what I call *emotional logic,* not intellectual logic. A person who tries to understand addiction using intellectual logic will become frustrated and feel manipulated by the addict. This is partly why talk therapy (talking one-on-one with only a counselor and without a support group) is so ineffective in convincing addicts to end their destructive, addictive relationships.

We can sum up emotional logic in the phrase "I want what I want and I want it now." Emotional needs often feel very urgent and compulsive. Emotional logic works to satisfy this urgency even if it is not in the best interest of the person.

For example, a compulsive gambler tells himself he is done gambling for the week. Shortly, however, he has a rough day at work and feels uneasy, so he looks over his racing form to try to ease his feelings, still telling himself he won't gamble anymore this week. While reviewing the racing form, he starts to hear his emotional logic telling him he has found a sure bet. "Why didn't I see this before?" he says. "It'd be crazy for me to miss this opportunity!" Thus, he becomes pitted against himself—one side believing in his "sure thing," the other reminding him of his promise not to gamble for the rest of the week. Inside, the emotional pressure builds. Because addiction involves the deep need to have emotional needs met and emotional pressures relieved, he finally must give in to his urge, especially after he has convinced himself he would be stupid not to grab this opportunity.

Emotional logic pits the addict against himself or herself. In the book *Alcoholics Anonymous,* there is a sentence that reads, "Remember that we deal with alcohol—cunning, baffling, powerful!" This is also one of the most truthful ways to describe the emotional logic found in all addictions: cunning, baffling, powerful.

Addiction Is More Than a Relationship of Convenience

Often, our relationships with objects or events are "relation-ships of convenience," meaning we manipulate objects for our own convenience to make our lives easier and more comfort-able. Most people have relationships of convenience with the same objects and events to which addicts get addicted—food, shopping, alcohol. Normally, these are relationships where there is no emotional bonding or illusion of intimacy. To ad-dicts, however, the object or event starts to become more and more important as they try to get their emotional and intimacy needs met through this relationship. Eventually, it becomes their *primary* emotional relationship. Because they experience a mood change, they start to believe their emotional needs have been met. This is an illusion.

Once a person starts to look to an object or event for emo-tional stability, he or she is building the foundation of an ad-dictive relationship with it. My definition of addiction, which is a variation of one developed in the chemical dependency field, is as follows: *addiction is a pathological love and trust re-lationship with an object or event.*

What exactly does this mean? To be pathological is to devi-ate from a healthy or normal condition. When someone is de-scribed as being ill, we mean that this person has moved away from what is considered "normal." The word *pathological,* therefore, means "abnormal"; consequently, addiction is an abnormal relationship with an object or event.

All objects have a normal, socially acceptable function: food is to nourish; gambling is for fun and excitement; drugs are to help manage pain or overcome illness. Anyone using these objects or events in these ways would be seen as having a normal, healthy relationship with them. In an addiction, however, the addict departs from the normal and socially ac-ceptable function of the object and sets up a pathological or abnormal relationship. The food, gambling, or drugs take on a new function: the addict develops a relationship with the event or object, hoping to get his or her needs met. This is the insanity of addiction, for people normally get emotional and intimacy needs met through a balanced combination of intimate connections with other people, themselves, their community, and with a Higher Power.

Addiction Is Not Reaching Out

These normal ways of achieving intimacy involve reaching out to life. We nurture ourselves by reaching out to others and then inward, to ourselves. In addiction, this reaching motion is almost totally inward to the point of withdrawing. Addiction exists within the person, and whenever addicts become preoccupied or act in addictive ways, this forces them to withdraw, to isolate themselves from others. The longer an addictive illness progresses, the less a person feels the ability to have meaningful relationships with others.

Addiction makes life very lonely and isolated, which creates more of a need for the addict to act out. When the addict hurts, he or she will act out by turning to the addiction for relief, just as someone else may turn to a spouse, a best friend, or spiritual beliefs. For the addict, the mood change created by acting out gives the illusion that a need has been met.

How Addicts Treat Themselves and Others

Because addiction is an illness in which the addict's primary relationship is with objects or events and not with people, the addict's relationships with people change to reflect this.

Normally, we manipulate objects for our own pleasure, to make life easier. Addicts slowly transfer this style of relating to objects to their interactions with people, treating them as one-dimensional objects to manipulate as well. For example, the sex addict sees people as sexual objects first and as people second. People around the addict get tired, frustrated, angry, and eventually fed up with being treated as objects. This leads to greater distance between others and the addict, who becomes even more isolated.

Addicts treat themselves as they treat others. In treating themselves as objects, addicts subject their emotions, mind, spirit, and body to many different dangers, including high levels of stress. As they continue to treat themselves as objects, they are often led to some form of breakdown.

Objects Are Predictable

Addicts begin to trust the addictive mood change caused by their addiction to an object or event because it's consistent and predictable. This is the seductive part of addiction.

- If you are a drug addict and you take a certain drug, you'll experience a predictable mood change.
- If you are addicted to gambling and you start to gamble, you'll experience a predictable mood change.
- If you are a compulsive eater, you'll experience a predictable mood change when you overeat.

The same goes for sex addicts, workaholics, addictive spenders, and people suffering from any other type of addiction—addiction causes them to experience a predictable mood change. Because addiction is predictable for addicts, they believe it can be trusted. Addicts rely upon a mood change, and the mood change comes through for them—in the beginning.

People, on the other hand, may not always come through. An addict may be in need of emotional support, so she goes to her best friend, only to find her in greater need of emotional support than the addict. When situations like this occur, the addict concludes that objects are more dependable than people.

If you were raised in an addictive or abusive family, you may have learned not to trust people. This will make you susceptible to the seductive illusion of comfort created by the predictable mood change offered by addiction.

Misplaced Priorities

Practicing addicts want to be first and demand to come first. Their wants become all-important. Objects have no wants or needs; thus, in a relationship with an object the addict can always come first. This quality is very attractive to the addict, and also fits well into the belief system created by emotional logic. A practicing addict comes to trust the addiction, not people. To trust in people is a threat to the addictive process. For the practicing addict, the object comes first, people second.

All of us want fulfillment and are looking for relationships that will give us this. Addiction is a relationship problem; it is a destructive but committed relationship. Like two people involved in a destructive relationship that makes no logical sense to others, yet goes on for years, the addict is having a destructive relationship with an object or event.

In its beginning stages, addiction is an attempt to emotionally fulfill oneself. In many ways, addiction is a normal process gone awry. Most friendships begin with emotional attachment and are based on getting emotional needs fulfilled. Addiction is a pathological way of trying to reach this fulfillment. A compulsive gambler is not chasing the win, though this is what he tells himself. What the addict trusts and depends on is the false promise and false sense of fulfillment produced by the preoccupation with gambling and the predictable mood change.

When Addictive Relationships Are Formed

There are times when all of us are susceptible to forming addictive relationships, such as after a great loss. With the loss comes pain and the need to replace the lost relationship. A good example of this is retirement, when the loss of a work relationship is often replaced by an addictive relationship. As people get older, friends pass away, and long-standing relationships start to change, many elderly people form addictive relationships with, for example, television or alcohol and other drugs. They come to trust in these objects, knowing they will be there tomorrow.

People may be susceptible to forming an addictive relationship at other times, as well:

- After the loss of a loved one (the closer the relationship the more likely the change).
- After a loss of status.
- After a loss of ideals or dreams.
- After the loss of friendships.
- When facing new social challenges or social isolation (for example, moving to a new community).
- When leaving one's family.

Seductiveness in Addiction

What makes the addictive relationship so attractive is the mood change it produces. It works every time; it's guaranteed. No human relationship can make this kind of guarantee. Addicts trust they will experience a mood change if they perform certain behaviors. For example, by gorging himself, the food addict can temporarily control his life and the way he feels. Thus, through acting out, the addict feels a sense of control. This helps to counteract the total sense of powerlessness and unmanageability the addict is feeling on a deeper, more personal level.

The addictive process is very seductive. Addiction is a process of buying into false and empty promises: the false promise of relief, the false promise of emotional security, the false sense of fulfillment, and the false sense of intimacy with the world. A compulsive gambler doesn't chase the event (gambling) itself, but what the event emotionally comes to represent—a symbol of fulfillment.

It is not only the relationship with a particular object that is dangerous for addicts; it's also dangerous to chase this form of dishonesty. Finding emotional fulfillment through an object or event is an illusion. It's dishonest to believe an object or event can bring anything more than a temporary mood change. Compulsive gamblers are not chasing the win. If the win was important, gamblers would stop when they won. They are chasing the action, the excitement, the moment, and eventually they chase the losing, for this allows them a reason to chase again. Continued dishonesty of this type can produce a new addictive relationship with another object, as objects can easily be replaced. Indeed highs come in many forms.

A friend of mine has a plaque on his wall that speaks well for the seduction of addiction.

Fooling people is serious business,
but when you fool yourself
it becomes fatal.

Intensity Mistaken for Intimacy

Emotionally, addicts get intensity and intimacy mixed up. Acting out is a very intense experience for addicts because it involves going against themselves.

- For compulsive eaters, buying a bag of groceries, eating most of the contents, and then making themselves throw up is a very intense experience.
- For sex addicts, entering pornographic bookstores and knowing they'll not leave before having sex with a complete stranger and knowing there's a chance they could be arrested is a very intense experience.
- For gambling addicts, watching a football game and knowing the team they have picked must win by six points so they can make a past-due house payment is a very intense experience.

During the trance created by acting out, addicts may feel very excited, very shameful, and very scared. Whatever they are feeling, they feel it intensely. Addicts feel very connected to the moment because of the intensity.

Intensity, however, is not intimacy, though addicts repeatedly get them mixed up. The addict has an intense experience and believes it is a moment of intimacy. For example, an alcoholic sees his relationships with drinking buddies as deep and very personal, but they slip away when the event of drinking doesn't occur.

I've learned a lot about the differences between intensity and intimacy from my fifteen-year-old niece, who is at an age where intensity and intimacy are often confused. She believes she is "totally in love" with a boy in her class, and is sure they will marry. She has already decided how many children they will have and what to name them. It would be an exercise in futility to try and talk her out of her emotional beliefs. All of us around her know she is misled by intensity. What she is feeling is very intense, but not very intimate.

Adolescence is a time of learning the differences between intensity and intimacy. Adolescents make promises of friendship for life and make extensive plans for the future based on this, only to see the friendships fade. Intimacy is something that is slowly built over time. Adolescents often have difficulty seeing beyond the moment.

Practicing addicts are also living for the present moment, using emotional logic. Emotionally, addicts act like adolescents and are often described as adolescent in behavior and attitude. After all, many issues addicts struggle with are the same issues that face adolescents. The difference is that addicts stay trapped in an adolescent stage as long as their illness is in progress.

Objects and Events That Become Addicting

What do different addictive objects and events (eating, gambling, chemicals, and sex) have in common? It's their ability to produce a positive and pleasurable mood change. This is the addictive potential of an object or event.

Both washing dishes and gambling are events, but for most people, washing dishes produces a much smaller pleasurable mood change. Milk and alcohol are substances, but people do not become addicted to milk because it does not have the same mood-changing quality as alcohol. Thus, the ability to produce a pleasurable mood change is needed for an object or event to have an addictive potential.

Availability of an object or event helps determine whether people will choose that form of addiction. The more available addictive objects or events are, the greater the number of people who form addictive relationships with them. Gambling is becoming more widely available; therefore, we are seeing a rise in the number of addictive gamblers.

A person can switch an addictive relationship from object to object and event to event. Switching from object to object helps create the illusion that the "problem has been taken care of," when in reality one addictive relationship has replaced another. This buys more time for the addict. An addict may stop using speed and pot and "just" take up drinking. Similarly, the recovering alcoholic who hasn't accepted his addictive relationship with alcohol may slowly develop an addictive relationship with food, putting on fifty or sixty pounds and remaining as emotionally isolated as he was when he was drinking.

Recovering and active addicts need to recognize that at times they will want to interact with the world through their addictions. When faced with stress, for example, addicts may want to reach for an object instead of reaching for people or their own spirituality to cope with the outside world.

Once an addictive relationship has developed, the active addict or recovering addict will always see the world in a different perspective. Like any other major illness, addiction is an experience that changes people in permanent ways. This is why it's so important that people in recovery attend Twelve Step and other self-help meetings on a regular basis; the addictive logic remains deep inside of them and looks for an opportunity to reassert itself in the same or a different form. Recovering addicts must continue to go to meetings and work the program because they continue to be addicts. Recovery is the continued acceptance of addiction and the continuous monitoring of the addictive personality in whatever form it may take.

Addiction must be viewed as a continuum because of its progressive nature. Some people teeter on a thin line between abuse and addiction for a long time. Addiction is different from periodic, or even frequent, abuse. This difference will become much more clear in the following pages that describe the *addictive personality:* the different changes that occur to addicts, their world, and the people who surround them as addiction develops.

P A R T 2

Stages of Addiction

Before we look at the three stages of addiction, let's discuss the concept of *process*. This book uses a process model to define addiction. Process involves movement, development, and change.

Process involves movement in a particular direction, much like a journey. It involves a beginning and possibly an end. Process is a flow, moving from one point to another in a particular direction. This direction may not always be totally clear, but it's there. Process is a set of experiences that indicate a particular change.

Addiction is such a set of experiences that indicate a specific movement in a specific direction, bringing a series of changes that take place within a person. It is through the commonalties of these experiences and changes that we are able to describe addiction.

As addiction develops, it becomes a way of life. Rather than being rigid, addiction is continually changing. As it changes, it inflicts changes on the person suffering from the addiction. As we study the stages of addiction, we will be looking at a particular process, a particular journey—the addictive process, the addictive journey.

Stage One: Internal Change

Long before anyone suspects or knows there is a problem, many changes will have taken place deep within the addict.

Addiction, like other major illnesses, changes people in permanent ways. In Stage One, a personality will be permanently altered. Addiction is so powerful that it can permanently alter a person's personality.

When people enter the addictive process, most either will continue in it for life or will reach a point where they, with the help of others, consciously choose another lifestyle called "recovery." Like many other diseases, addiction grows and develops within, long before it reaches a stage where it is recognized by the addict and others.

How It Begins

The journey starts when the addict experiences the high—the mood change—produced by certain behaviors with objects or events.

- The journey for compulsive gamblers starts when they feel a mood change caused by the excitement of a first win.
- The journey for compulsive spenders starts when they find their moods can be changed by purchasing something.
- The journey for alcoholics starts when they get intoxicated for the first time and find that a substance can make them feel different.
- The journey for anorexics starts when they experience the sense of control brought about by not eating.

All of us, even those who are not addicts, experience similar mood changes; but to the prospective addict, it is new, intense knowledge. In the mood change exists the illusion of control, the illusion of comfort, and the illusion of perfection. For the addict, these mood change experiences are often very intense. Research in the areas of alcohol and gambling addictions shows that the addicted person's first few experiences are often very enjoyable and very intense; therefore, the intoxication experience is very profound. For example, early on in their experiences, many compulsive gamblers have had a "big win" or have been with someone who has had a "big win." There are also many alcoholics who can describe in great detail their first drinking experiences long after they have occurred. For the addict, this intensity gets mistaken for intimacy, self-esteem, social comfort, or any number of things.

Intoxicating experiences bring the knowledge that through a relationship with an object or event, one's feelings can change. People turn toward addictive or compulsive behavior when they don't like the way they're feeling, and they seek out a mood-changing experience. Not everyone who seeks a mood change becomes an addict. Some people will abuse objects or events for a period of time and then turn to other, healthier ways of getting their needs met. Nevertheless, in turning to an object or event for relief, one finds the basic illusion upon which addiction is based: finding relief through objects.

Natural Relationships

There are natural relationships people need to turn to for support, nurturing, guidance, love, and emotional and spiritual growth.

1. *Family and friends.* We get day-to-day intimacy needs met through relationships with family and friends. We develop a better sense of ourselves through feedback from these people. It's also through our relationships with family and friends that we develop a sense of importance to others, and a sense of being needed as we need others. We learn how to help others and how

others can help us. We also learn a sense of responsibility, knowing that how we act affects others and how others act affects us. In our relationships with family and friends, we learn how to have healthy interdependencies.

2. *Spiritual Higher Power.* In our spiritual lives, we believe in a power outside of ourselves, greater than ourselves. The definition of this power varies from person to person. For some, a spiritual Higher Power is a religious God; for others, God is nature or a close, supportive group of friends. Through a relationship with a spiritual Higher Power we learn to perceive and accept a natural order, a natural flow. We learn to see the important space we inhabit within the world and among other living beings, but we also learn that we're only one piece of humanity. With this perspective, we learn how to view the world and ourselves with a sense of realism. We also develop a relationship we can turn to when family or friends are not enough or can't be there for some reason. We learn to believe in and trust something greater than ourselves. We learn to have faith, which means we don't have to live only for the moment. We believe and trust there will be future moments of serenity and a sense of well-being.

3. *Self.* Through a caring relationship with ourselves we learn self-nurturing—the ability to love ourselves and see ourselves as one resource we can turn to during times of difficulty. It's through a relationship with ourselves that we learn the most about change, either positive or negative. As we watch and interact with ourselves, we see our vast potential for change. It's through a caring relationship with ourselves that we learn to be caring and patient with others. The rela-

tionship we have with ourselves is carried in some
form to all our other relationships.

4. *Community.* Through our relationship with the different communities we live in (our home community, our
work community, and a recovering community), we
learn about responsibility for ourselves and others. We
learn to view relationships within a large framework:
we learn to contribute; we learn to take; we learn to
give and receive care from those we have never met;
and we learn to be interdependent.

If people do not develop relationships within these four
groups, they turn to other types of relationships. This is where
addiction comes in. Addiction is a relationship with an object
or event that takes place within the person. What all four types
of relationships have in common is the fact that people must
reach within themselves, but they must also reach out. In natural relationships there is a connecting with others—an act of
giving and an act of receiving. In addiction there is only an act
of taking. Natural relationships are based on emotionally connecting with others; addiction is based on emotional isolation.

The Addictive Cycle

Any addictive relationship begins when a person repeatedly
seeks the illusion of relief to avoid unpleasant feelings or situations. This is nurturing through avoidance—an unnatural way
of taking care of one's emotional needs. At this point, addicts
start to give up natural relationships and the relief they offer.
They replace these relationships with the addictive relationship.

Consequently, addicts seek serenity through an object or
event. This is the beginning of the addictive cycle, as illus-
trated in a diagram that depicts addictions as a downward spiral with many valleys and plateaus.

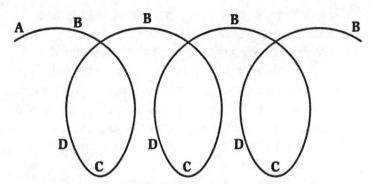

A = pain; B = feel the need to act out; C = act out, start to feel better; D = pain resulting from acting out; B = feel the need to act out; C = act out, start to feel better.

This cycle causes an emotional craving that results in mental preoccupation. For an addict, the feeling of discomfort becomes a signal to act out, not a signal to connect with others or with oneself. The amount of mental obsession is often an indication of the stress in the addict's life. Some addictions produce physical dependency that creates physical symptoms upon withdrawal (as with alcohol and other drugs). Many other types of recovering addicts—sex addicts, addictive gamblers, and addictive spenders—also report physical symptoms when they stop acting out. This may be part of the grief process that takes place when ending an addictive relationship, or actual withdrawal symptoms, or a combination of both. Addicts who have stopped acting out report feeling edgy and nervous, and these symptoms can last anywhere from a few days up to a few months.

The Addictive Personality

It needs to be made very clear that the addictive personality I speak of gets created from the illness of addiction and represents a change resulting from the addictive process that takes place within a person. This personality does not exist prior to the illness of addiction, nor does it represent a predisposition to addiction; rather, it emerges from the addictive process. In the same way that cancer or other long-term illnesses can alter one's personality, the illness of addiction also can affect an individual's life and personality. This is what I mean when I use the term *addictive personality*.

The most important aspect of Stage One is the creation of this addictive personality: the Self and the Addict. The Self represents the "normal," human side of the addicted person, while the Addict represents the side that is consumed and transformed by the addiction. Eventually, the addicted person forms a dependent relationship with his or her own addictive personality. The following quote from Robert Louis Stevenson's *Dr. Jekyll and Mr. Hyde* provides an accurate illustration of these two sides of the addict's personality. In this quote, Dr. Jekyll describes the loss of his "Self."

> . . . whereas in the beginning the difficulty had been to throw off the body of Jekyll, it had of late gradually but decidedly transferred itself to the other side . . . I was slowly losing hold of my original and better self and becoming slowly incorporated with my second and worse self.

Once an addictive personality is established within a person, the specific object or event of the addiction takes on less importance. When the Addict is firmly in control, addicted people can (and often do) switch objects of addiction as preferences change or as trouble arises with one particular object or event. Addicts who switch objects of addiction also know it's a good way to get people off their backs.

The Addict side of the personality is very important for recovering addicts to understand because it will stay with them for life. On some level, the Addict will always be searching for an object or some type of event with which to form an addictive relationship. On some level, this personality will always want to give the person the illusion that there is an object or event that can nurture him or her.

The term *dry drunk* describes a person whose life is being controlled by an addictive personality despite abstinence from substance use, gambling, sexual acting out, and so on. Dry drunks still trust in the addictive process and cut themselves off from the natural forms of relationships they need to be nurtured. People in a recovery program for alcohol addiction, for example, need to clearly understand that they are prone to form a possible addictive relationship with another object or event, such as food or gambling. For these people, sobriety acquires a new dimension: instead of only monitoring their relationship with alcohol, they also need to learn how to monitor the addictive part of themselves.

In the example of alcohol and food addiction, it's possible for a recovering alcoholic to, within three or four years of leaving an alcoholism treatment center, gain forty or fifty pounds and be as unhappy and emotionally isolated as he was the day he entered treatment. As one such person stated, "I now find myself eating for all the same reasons I drank: I'm lonely, I'm afraid." Many of these people attend AA regularly, are working good recovery programs, and find their lives are much less crisis-centered, but something stands in their way of serenity—another addiction.

It's in understanding the addictive personality, even in recovery, that the words *cunning, baffling, powerful* show their true meaning. It's the addictive relationship inside oneself that the recovering person will need to acknowledge and break, not just the relationship with an object. This is where total recovery takes place.

Development of the Addict

The foundation of the addict is found in all people. It's found in a normal desire to make it through life with the least amount of pain and the greatest amount of pleasure possible. It's found in our negativity and our mistrust of others and the world, whether this pessimism is valid or not. There is nothing wrong with this part of us; it's natural to have these beliefs to some degree. However, when these beliefs control one's way of life, as they do in addiction, people get into trouble. Some people are more susceptible to addiction than others; these are people who don't know how to have healthy relationships and have been taught not to trust. They may have been treated badly by others while growing up, and never learned good relationship skills as a result.

If you were raised in a family where closeness was not a reality, you are much more prone to form an addictive relationship, for two reasons: first, you were taught to distance yourself from people, not connect with them; second, growing up in this type of family left you with a deep, lonely emptiness that you've wanted to have filled. Addiction offers the illusion of such fulfillment. If you were raised in a family where people were treated as objects rather than as people, you have already been taught addictive logic. In this case, recovery is not a return to a healthier self, but a need to develop a new personality.

Addiction is an active belief in and a commitment to a negative lifestyle. Addiction begins and grows when a person abandons the natural ways of getting emotional needs met— through connecting with other people, one's community, one's self, and spiritual powers greater than oneself. The repeated abandonment of oneself and one's values in favor of the addictive high causes the addictive personality to develop and gradually gain power.

The negative reinforcement of an addictive personality is similar to a person who gets up each morning and throughout the day says to herself, "Why bother? Life is hard." The more she tells herself this, the more she will develop the lifestyle and personality of someone who has given up on life. Every time addicts choose to act out in an addictive way, they are saying to themselves one or more of the following:

- I don't really need people.
- I don't have to face anything I don't want to.
- I'm afraid to face life and my problems.
- Objects and events are more important than people.
- I can do anything I want, whenever I want, no matter whom it hurts.

This type of thinking continually supports and reinforces an addictive belief system in an addict. A personality change begins to take place. In most cases these changes are subtle and happen gradually, which explains in part the seductiveness of the addictive process.

Shame

As time goes on and a person continues to act out, be preoccupied, and remain emotionally distant from others, the Addict side of his or her personality starts to assert more control over that person's internal life. At this stage, the person suffering from addiction will start to feel a "pull" inside. This may come in the form of emotional restlessness or pangs of conscience.

Addiction now starts to produce shame as a by-product. This happens both consciously and unconsciously to addicts, but mostly on an unconscious level. The more addicts seek relief through addiction, the more shame they'll start to experience and the more they will feel a need to justify the addictive relationship to themselves.

Shame creates a loss of *self*-respect, *self*-esteem, *self*-confidence, *self*-discipline, *self*-determination, *self*-control, *self*-importance, and *self*-love. In the beginning, this shame may be a general uneasiness; it's the first cost an addict pays for the addictive relationship. The addict starts to feel shame about the signs of loss of control that are beginning to appear within, more on an emotional, thinking level than behaviorally. This is typical in Stage One. The addict is more apt to feel bad about the internal withdrawal from others, for as addicts slowly start to become more committed to an object or event, they begin to emotionally withdraw from intimate relationships with self, others, and a Higher Power.

Where the Addictive Personality Emerges

Addiction starts to create pain, the very thing the person is trying to avoid. In creating pain, the process also creates a need for the continuation of the addictive relationship. *The addict seeks refuge from the pain of addiction by moving further into the addictive process.* The addict seeks happiness and serenity in the high or trance, but because the addict has started to withdraw from himself or herself and others, the addict can't see that the pain he or she feels is created by acting out.

Long before episodes of being out of control behaviorally appear, the person has fought and lost many battles on the emotional level, where the addictive personality develops and slowly gains control. This is the first part of the addict's personality that becomes controlled by the addictive process.

Addicts act like kids—if it feels good, they do it. They explore; they follow the emotional impulses that come from the very core of their beings instead of logic. At this stage, the person may feel uneasy, restless, and guilty. These are internal warning signals, but part of the addictive process is learning how to deny these warning signals. Addiction is also a process of denial—denial of reality, but mainly denial of the self. This denial must be accomplished for the addiction to progress.

"Talk therapy" hasn't proven very effective in treating addicts, for the core of the illness exists on an emotional level, not on a thinking level.

How the Addictive Personality Gains Control

Much of an addict's mental obsession results from denial or refusing to recognize the loss of control that is happening on an emotional level. Avoiding the reality of a situation and betraying one's humanity allow the creation of more pain, which will eventually create the need to explain to oneself what is happening. This will evolve into obsessive thoughts or preoccupation and rationalizations. The obsessive thoughts begin to occur more often and consist of constant questioning: *Why?* Preoccupation has to do with acting out and creating a mood change.

We've all heard the saying, "Just change your thoughts and you'll feel better." No one knows this better than addicts. If practicing addicts don't like the way they're feeling, all they need to do is think about acting out and a subtle mood change occurs. Each time this happens, the person loses a small piece of control that is transferred to the addiction.

We are starting to see how the gradual loss of the Self occurs in addiction, and how the Addict slowly gains more and more control. *The decrease in Self causes an increase in the addictive personality.*

In addiction, there is an almost constant internal conflict between the Self and the Addict. In this struggle, the Addict invariably wins. This is what is meant by "loss of control." The longer the struggle, the more control the addictive personality gains and establishes. Each time the Self struggles against the addiction, the Addict becomes stronger. To fight and struggle against something that has more power than oneself drains one's energy. For each defeat there is some loss of self-esteem. This is why people are taught to surrender in recovery. It is through accepting that one can't conquer the disease that the person finds the strength to start connecting with others.

Everybody has a dream. It may be as simple as having good friends, family, and a peaceful life. Every Addict also has a dream, a dream to escape pain and enter a "peaceful" trance-like state caused by acting out in an addictive manner.

The Self also has its own dream. In addiction, the Addict's dream clashes with the Self's dream, and the Self begins to lose control. The intimate relationship the Self was hoping to have with a friend starts to be replaced by food, gambling, sex, or alcohol. Addicts find themselves acting and saying things that distance them from the people they love.

As Stage One continues, the Self and Addict continue to fight for control:

- The Addict develops its own way of feeling.
- The Self disapproves of the Addict's beliefs, but enjoys the mood change.
- The Addict develops its own way of thinking.
- The Self regularly fights and argues with the Addict, but loses.
- The Addict develops its own way of behaving.
- The Self makes promises to control the Addict, uses willpower to control the Addict, then works to contain the Addict, but eventually becomes dependent on the Addict's personality.

The addictive relationship is an internal relationship between the Self and the Addict; it is a one-to-one relationship

based on emotional logic. It creates an inward focus and isolation, and is sustained by the mood change produced by acting out in the addictive process. This relationship increases
shame and the defense of denial. The longer the interaction
between the Self and the Addict, the stronger the addictive personality becomes; the longer the interaction, the more developed the addictive relationship within becomes. Over time, the
Addict becomes the dominant personality.

Friends and family members often desperately ask themselves and others, "Why does he act like this? Doesn't he care
about us anymore?" The truth is that the Addict within does
not care about them. What it cares about is acting out and
achieving the trance. The Addict doesn't care about the Self either. A statement such as, "At least if you won't stop for me,
stop for yourself!" falls on deaf ears. The person who suffers
from an addiction often asks the same questions long before
anyone else: "Why do I act this way? Don't I care?"

Many families have gathered together in tears, realizing it's
the Addict, the illness, the addiction they all hate and fear, not
the person. It's often a great relief for people suffering from an
addiction to realize that they are not "bad people" as they believed, that their addictive personality is not all of them, but
only a part of them that has grown as a result of the illness.

The Illusion of Control

We have seen that, over time, the Addict side of the personality develops its own way of feeling, thinking, and behaving.
When people act out, they get high and feel different, and this
changes their thought patterns. Any feeling that creates discomfort becomes a signal to act out; internal clues of discomfort start to become internal clues to act out. When a food addict feels sadness, for example, the Addict will sense this
sadness and interpret it not as a real feeling, but as a clue

about food. Thus, the person's feelings become mental obsessions. In Stage One, the person repeatedly chooses this pattern of distorted interpretation of real sensations.

Why does an addicted person make that choice? By choosing an addictive interpretation of a feeling, the person gets an illusion of control. Addicts chase control—they believe they will find peace and happiness through total or perfect control. However, it's human to be imperfect and powerless, and chasing the illusion of control is really running away from the reality of being human. Addicts seek perfection instead of humanity.

Addicts will make addictive choices when they are feeling powerless, helpless, or weak. The addictive choice creates a feeling of being in control and closer to perfection, at least for a while. Trying to gain that feeling of control, even if it is just an illusion, is very tempting. Accepting the reality of one's powerlessness is difficult to do.

Addictive Logic

At times, the person feels something is wrong and senses the danger of making the addictive choice. Internally, a person starts to question the pathological relationship that is beginning to form. It is due to this questioning that addictive thinking, or what I call *addictive logic,* starts to develop. Addictive logic develops as a person tries to justify the subtle changes that are starting to take place within. The first person to experience personal change is the person to whom it is happening. The person may be the last to *acknowledge* the change, but is the first to experience it.

It's through the development of addictive logic that the addicted person finds a way to cope with the changes within. A food addict will start to question internal urges to eat more often. In the very beginning, these urges are simply and quickly dismissed. As their frequency increases, the person starts to explain them away using addictive logic. "It's just something I like to do while watching television." "I only eat like this occasionally." "I'd better get my fill since I'll start my diet tomorrow."

Addictive logic is not based on truth, but on the delusion of the addictive relationship. Addictive logic denies the presence of an addictive relationship. The addicted person comes to believe that the problem exists elsewhere or is too big to overcome. An addictive gambler may see herself as having a marriage problem, not a gambling problem, thus the addictive relationship continues. A food addict may believe he has no control over what he puts in his mouth, and becomes helpless to do anything about it.

It may make no sense that some people eat themselves into loneliness, gamble away their homes, drink away their livers, have sex with total strangers, or take a drug not even knowing what it is. An understanding of addictive logic can shed light on the cause of such behavior. Most people, and even those who suffer from addiction, try to make sense of addictive behavior by using normal logic. This does not work.

Normal logic tells us it's not right to hurt one's Self; addictive logic says it is all right to hurt one's Self because the Self is not important—it's the mood change or trance that counts.

Normal logic tells us it's not right to hurt others; addictive logic says it is all right to hurt others because relationships with people are not important. What is important is a relationship with an object or event.

By using addictive logic instead of normal logic, we start to see and understand an addicted person's personality. When an alcoholic says, "I truly don't care what you think of my drinking," one gets a sense of an addict's view of relationships. When the addict says, "I'm not hurting anyone but myself," one gets a true glimmer of the addict's feelings and beliefs about the Self.

Keep in mind that in Stage One, the addictive personality seems less frightening and more of a friend. This forms the basis for what is known as *euphoric recall*—remembering the pleasurable aspects of the addictive process and denying or forgetting the pain. In Stage One, acting out and experiencing the mood change creates fun, excitement, new ideas, and stimulation. It is not until Stage Two that the acting out starts to lose some of its seductiveness. The object or event always retains its ability to change one's mood, but over time much of the fun starts to vanish and the acting out takes on a maintenance quality—the person acts out more and more to cover up and escape from the pain and frustration created by the addictive process.

The Addictive Delusion System

Slowly over time, addictive logic develops into a belief system—a delusion system from which the addicted person's life will be directed. The person will fight this and delay it as long as possible, but eventually the delusion system and the Addict take control.

As the illness progresses, the delusion system will become more complex and rigid. The delusion system is commonly described as a wall surrounding the person, one that has two main functions. First, it keeps one locked inside oneself with only the Addict to relate to. An addicted person's world is a lonely one; his or her focus is directed inward. If a person tries to break from the addictive world, he or she is confronted with the addictive delusion system. When addicts ask themselves, "When is this going to stop?" they hear an idle promise of the Addict within saying, "It's not that bad."

The second function of the delusion system is to keep away people who would endanger the addictive relationship.

During a crisis, a crack often appears in the delusion system, allowing the addict's Self and concerned others to connect with the addicted person and provide help. Within a day or two, however, this crack repairs itself and the delusion system regains control. Often, the addicted person is not able to remember what happened.

When Recovery Takes Place

By accepting and taking responsibility for the presence of an addictive personality, addicted people can start recovery and begin to choose relationships that allow them to move outside of themselves. True acceptance of the presence and strength of an addictive personality forces addicts to seek help outside of themselves.

The first step in recovery is the acceptance of the dual personalities created in addiction. By accepting the two sides of their addiction, people often create a door that opens outward, allowing them to establish healthy relationships. This frees them from shame. In recovery, the person will need to take total responsibility for both the Self and the Addict. Denial of an addictive personality is part of a practicing addict's life. Thus, admitting the presence of the addiction is the basis for recovery.

By acknowledging and claiming the Addict side of his or her personality and then coming to understand and listen for addictive logic, the addicted person enters into recovery. Programs of recovery stress being totally honest with one's Self, and listening to and believing in one's Self, not one's Addict.

Stage Two: Lifestyle Change

Once the addictive personality is firmly in place, the behavioral aspects of addiction become more prevalent. The behavior of addicted people is the most visible part of addiction and thus the easiest to focus attention on. Addictive behavior—such as addictively overspending, compulsively going to pornographic bookstores, and bingeing on and purging food—regularly occurs only after the development of the addictive personality. These behaviors are all signs that the person is out of control on an internal level. In Stage Two, the person also becomes out of control on a behavioral level.

In Stage One, the addicted person is able to contain addiction to the degree that there are few episodes of being behaviorally out of control. In Stage Two, these episodes become more and more frequent as the person becomes much more preoccupied with the object or event. It is in this stage that others start to notice that something is wrong or abnormal. Others start to see the presence of the Addict.

In Stage One, the person behaved mainly within socially acceptable limits. The addictive gambler gambled mostly within acceptable limits; the food addict ate mostly within normal limits; the alcoholic drank socially most of the time. But inside all of these people, there starts to develop a deep and totally consuming mental dependency.

In Stage Two, a *behavioral dependency* starts to develop. In behavioral dependency, a person starts to act out the addictive belief system in a ritualistic manner, and the person's behavior becomes more and more out of control. Once an addictive personality has established control emotionally and mentally, the person becomes dependent on the addictive personality, not on the mood change or the object or event. The addictive belief system becomes a person's foundation, and it develops into a lifestyle.

It is in this stage that addicts start to arrange their lives and relationships using addictive logic to guide them. In Stage Two, the behavioral commitment to the addictive process has become all-encompassing.

The Addict's Behavior

There are many ways a person's behavior adapts to the addictive process, bringing about an addictive lifestyle. Betrayal of Self and others becomes a regular occurrence:

- The person starts to lie to others, even when it is easier to tell the truth.
- The person starts to blame others, knowing others are not to blame.
- The person starts to ritualize his or her behavior.
- The person starts to withdraw from others.

Not only will the person have a secret world to withdraw to emotionally and mentally, but also a physical secret world in which he or she lives out an addictive lifestyle:

- It is in this stage that food addicts may start hiding food or starving themselves.
- It is in this stage that sex addicts may start going to prostitutes or having multiple affairs.
- It is in this stage that addictive gamblers may open secret bank accounts or get secret jobs.
- It is in this stage that alcoholics may begin to have a couple of quick shots and a few breath mints before going home.

Each of these examples shows a behavioral commitment to the addictive process. Each time people act out in these ways, they are depending more on the addictive process and its logic and less on themselves and others who love them.

Addicts must make sense of this to themselves, and they do so by denying the fear and pain caused by their inappropriate behavior. This is where the addict turns to denial, repression, lies, rationalizations, and other defenses to help cope with what is happening.

Thus, whenever addicts act out and then explain their actions away, they unintentionally deepen their commitment to addiction. Whenever addicts act out, they must emotionally and mentally withdraw into the addictive personality to receive support for acting out. This inward motion isolates them from the world and others around them, causing them to lose more of their humanity. This creates loneliness and a longing to reach out and connect, which internally becomes another signal to act out.

The addictive process has the power and ability to create a need for itself. Through repeated acting out combined with mental obsession, another form of commitment to the Addict will now steadily establish more and more control. The behavioral loss of control is an expression of the internal loss of control by the Self to the Addict.

Examples of Addictive Promises

Addict: "Bring me your pain, I will give you relief."
Translation: "Bring me your pain, I'll give you the illusion of relief."

Addict: "I will set you free."
Translation: "I will come to own you."

Addict: "Spend time with me, you can trust me. You can't trust anyone else."
Translation: "Spend time with me, I'll teach you to be mistrustful of others."

Addict: "I'll teach you a way in which you won't have to face issues."
Translation: "You can hide temporarily, but the issues won't go away."

Addictive Rituals

Rituals are important for many reasons. Rituals help to bind us to our beliefs and values, and connect us to others with similar beliefs and values. We reassure ourselves of our beliefs and values through our use of rituals. Whenever we are involved in a ritual, it will strengthen our ties to whatever it represents.

Erich Fromm states in his book *The Sane Society* that in a ritual, a person "acts out with his body what he thinks out with his brain." Rituals are value statements. In addiction, rituals become value statements about the beliefs of the Addict. These rituals can be, and often are, totally opposite from the beliefs of the Self. Therefore, in addiction the addicted person acts out with his or her body the addictive logic existing in the brain.

Rituals are a form of language—a language of behavior. Rituals speak about our faith and about our current beliefs and values, either positive or negative. For example, participating in the ritual of a family birthday party can help tie us to our family. Many aspects of this ritual are predictable: who will arrive on time and who will arrive late, who will make the dumb jokes at the wrong times, and who will engage in serious conversation. Our involvement in this ritual becomes a statement, especially to ourselves about what we believe is important. Even if we don't want to participate, we feel it's important that we do. We have acted "right" by taking part.

Our actions also are prescribed by the ritual itself. When the ritual is a birthday party, people sing "Happy Birthday," smile, make certain comments to the person having the birthday, bring presents, and eat certain foods.

When addicts are involved in addictive rituals and behaviors, they, too, act in prescribed ways. They are making behavioral statements that support the addictive process and addictive belief system, just like attending a family birthday party is making a behavioral statement in support of one's family and the family's belief system.

Besides binding us to beliefs and values and to others with similar beliefs, rituals bring us comfort because they are predictable. Rituals are based on consistency: first you do this, then you do that. The comfort may not always be apparent, but it is there. When the sequence of the ritual is changed or part of the sequence is left out, we experience discomfort. Addicts ritualize their behavior for the comfort found in predictability. Addicts also ritualize their actions around behaviors they find exciting; they feel comfortable knowing the excitement will be there if they act in certain ways.

Rituals bring us comfort at times of crisis or during times of conflict. By engaging in ritualized behavior, we are brought back to our beliefs and experience the comfort that we find within them. When our lives are in turmoil, we tend to seek out consistency and familiarity. Addicts do the same: when they face crisis and stress, they run to the comfort they find in their rituals. Addictive rites tie them not only to a belief or value, but also to a mood—a feeling in which they've come to have faith and find comfort.

Rituals are statements about what people have faith in. Addicts no longer put faith in people, but in their addictive rite. Each part of the rite is important to the Addict and is designed to heighten the mood change.

Addicts also have their rituals of preference. One sex addict began on his way home from work. He would stop at a store and buy a pornographic magazine. Arriving home, he would pour himself a drink, then sit and slowly look through the magazine. After a couple of drinks, and after reaching a certain level of excitement, he would put on his acting-out clothes (a specific outfit in which he felt sexually attractive). He would leave home and go to a topless bar for another couple of drinks. Next, he would cruise certain parts of town looking for prostitutes. He would talk with them, bargaining back and forth, but would not have sex with them. Then he would go to a porno shop and look through magazines. On the way home, he would stop at his favorite sauna parlor and have sex with one of the prostitutes working there. He would go home feeling shameful and promise himself he would never do this again.

He would act out this ritual two or three times a month. Each part of the ritual had a certain meaning to him and was dependent on the part that preceded it. For example, he would not have sex with the street prostitutes because he saw himself as being above that. Because of his addictive logic, this part of his ritual helped him feel less shameful about his behavior.

Choices and Rituals

It is through our rituals and the faith we have in them that we hope to solve the internal conflict we feel when we are faced with choices. When we act according to a ritual, we have made a choice to do so. When facing a choice, a person with an addiction feels a great tension inside: *Do I act out or don't I act out?* This tension can go on for hours, days, or weeks at a time, and is a large part of the suffering caused by addiction. The addictive ritual will ease this tension, for when an addict is involved in a ritual, this conflict is momentarily over; a choice has been made and there is a sense of release.

Addicts may then face a different type of stress or tension, one caused by the shame of acting out. But the internal tension of *do I act out or don't I?* has been solved for the moment. This release of tension is shown in the example given earlier; the sex addict would internally debate whether or not to act out as he drove home every night. Most often he would make it home safely, but as soon as he made the decision to stop at that first store and buy a porno magazine, his Addict took over. He felt at ease at that moment, for the internal struggle between Self and Addict was over. He had surrendered to his addiction, and his release of tension and sense of peace helped to reinforce the choosing of the addictive process. This is called *negative surrendering.*

The Community and Rituals

The community to which we become tied will give us direction and rules of conduct. The rituals we perform will always tie us to some community, even if we perform the rituals alone. If we say a certain prayer in private, it will help tie us to the group that uses and believes in that prayer.

Addictive rituals most often take place alone or within a group whose members have no real caring connection to each other. Most often the group's only connection is their common form of acting out.

Addictive relationships are very superficial and are very private. The Addict is given complete control. The Addict inside does not care to be with people, but prefers to be alone or with other addicts who know, accept, and are not scared by their rites of addiction:

- The alcoholic drinks alone or with "drinking buddies."
- The bulimic's rite of bingeing and purging is a private act, but in another way this ritual is still a tie to a community whose members are secret to each other. Perhaps they will only meet when they band together in recovery to help each other fight their common enemy, food addiction.
- The addictive gambler most often prefers to be alone, but can recognize other addicts by the way they act, the symbols they carry, and the places they meet. They

often pass each other, recognizing each other's presence in a silent way; if they talk, it is about their common interest in gambling.
- The sex addict goes to the X-rated movie theater only to be alone in a private, addictive world. If there is acting out with someone, it often takes place without words, but with addictive looks to communicate who will do what in the addictive rite.

Addiction is a negative form of worship through connection with one's negative side, the Addict, at the expense of the Self. The Self witnesses the addictive ritual and is often sickened by what it is forced to participate in, but it is held captive by the power of the disease.

Commitment and Rituals

The purpose of any ritual is to deepen one's commitment, to move a person deeper into a certain view of the world. Addictive rituals also have this purpose, pushing a person deeper into the addictive process. Each time a person acts out, his or her addictive belief and defense system is strengthened. People who suffer from addictions must turn to addictive systems (using addictive logic) to explain away their actions; otherwise, they would find these actions hard to accept.

Our culture is made up of many groups, and each group has its own rituals with rules of conduct that bind its members together. This is no different for addictive rituals. Participating in the rituals of a group is a sign of membership within that group. If a person performs a certain behavior, then that person is a member of a certain group.

There are often initiation rites into a group. When I was a child, my friends and I formed a secret club. As we were initiated into the club, we were taught how to make a certain sign as a way for us to recognize one another. Whenever we would see each other at any club meeting or on the street, the sign was given and we would feel special and included. Our commitment to our club was strengthened. We believed in our club and the friendship for which it stood. As we grew older and our interest in secret clubs started to fade, our use of "the sign" faded away too, but we found other ways to show our friendship.

I'm sure if I were to see any of these friends today and show them the sign there would be smiles, and conversation of old memories would follow. For a moment we would be connected to each other as club members again. Our ritual did have a power that bound us as friends. The sign represented our commitment to each other—it was a statement about our relationship and importance to each other.

For addicts, the object of their addiction becomes a symbol of their relationship to the world. It is a statement that, at this time, they are choosing relationships with objects or events over people and spiritual relationships. Every time the addict is engaged in an addictive ritual, the object or event takes on more power. As a symbol, the object gains more and more power. Addicts become fanatics about their rituals:

- Food becomes a powerful symbol for the food addict.
- Sex or anything sexual is all-powerful for the sex addict.
- For the alcoholic, the use of alcohol comes to be a part of sacred ritual, more powerful than life itself.

Developing Healthy Rituals

All addicts develop some form of rigid ritualistic acting out. It is important for recovering people to understand their Addict has preferred ways of acting out, and that there are danger areas, times, and behavior they need to avoid. A recovering spending addict who has a ritual of acting out on Friday evenings will need to make sure he is around safe friends doing safe activities on Friday nights for some time to come. A sex addict who cruised a certain part of town as part of her addictive ritual will need to stay away from that part of town.

Healthy rituals bind us to others, to family or friends, to helpful spiritual principles, or to a community based on helping each other. In this sense, *addictive rituals are reverse rituals:* their primary purpose is to isolate us from others. Healthy rituals help us feel better about ourselves; addictive rituals make us feel worse about ourselves. Healthy rituals bind us to people who care for us; addictive rituals bind us to the Addict of the dangerous side of others. Healthy rituals help us have better relationships; addictive rituals destroy relationships. Healthy rituals help us to feel pride about ourselves and friends; addictive rituals cause shame. Healthy rituals are about celebrating life; addictive rituals seek out death.

Inner Struggle

A person suffering from addiction believes he or she should be able to control the addiction; thus, each time the person acts out, the Self feels more shameful. Most often, the Self disapproves of the Addict's belief system and its treatment of others, but has lost control and is unable to stop this process. It is in Stage Two that the person starts to sense and eventually surrenders to the immense power of addiction.

In Stage Two, the addicted person tries to establish behavioral limits, but that also doesn't work. This causes more shame and eventual surrender to the presence of the addiction.

Before surrender occurs, however, the person starts to work to contain the addiction, directing much energy inward to the addictive relationship. This causes more isolation. A practicing addict is an emotional loner, truly preferring to be alone. The presence of other people—especially someone who wants to be close—is an annoyance. But at the same time the Self can be craving a human connection—someone who can help with and listen to what is happening.

People Problems

As the illness progresses and the addicted person becomes more and more inwardly directed, others surrounding the person will sense this emotional withdrawal and react to it. This will be the start of "people problems" for the addict.

Since an addict's primary emotional attachment is to an object or event and not to people, many changes take place in the addict's life. Addicts start to manipulate other people and treat them as objects. Not surprisingly, it doesn't make much sense to them that others are offended by this. The Addict is often very self-righteous and self-centered.

One addicted person lied to his wife about his behavior and went into a rage when she dared to question him. He asked, "Why should I talk with my spouse if she isn't going to believe me when I say something?" This complaint would be justifiable in a normal relationship, but his addiction caused an abnormal relationship.

To the addict, other people's concern is seen as a problem. People are seen as nosy, and their concern becomes an obstacle to be overcome. People—including the Self part of the personality—are unimportant unless they can be used to deepen the addiction. If not, they are discarded.

Another reason addicts find comfort in having a primary emotional relationship with objects or events instead of people is because objects or events can't ask questions. Objects will never complain about the way the addict acts, and objects don't appear to make demands. These aspects of the addictive world become more and more attractive as the illness progresses and the addict's mistrust of others grows.

In this stage, if family or friends try to connect with the person to find out what is happening, they will be met with some form of resistance—often a lie, silent withdrawal, or even a personal attack.

Addicts start to mistrust others in Stage Two because they project their belief systems and addictive values on everyone else. The addictive belief system assumes that people use each other (because people are just objects) and that "you must do unto others before they do unto you." Most people who suffer from addiction intellectually reject this belief, but they have no emotional resources to fight it. The Self is no longer in control; the Addict is. This causes more shame, and they often start to feel victimized, sorry for themselves, and despairing. They often look for someone or something to blame as the villain, and it usually ends up being someone close.

The saddest part is that, in reality, it's the addicted person who is the victim. Like any other illness, addiction is an assault against a person, but the addict is unable to see this. For an addict to see what is happening as the result of addiction could be seen as a threat to acting out. Most often, the anger and stress addicts feel is projected toward others first, then themselves, and finally the whole world.

The attacks, the withdrawal, the lying, and the denial are all, at this point, acting-out behaviors. It's through these forms of acting out that internal pain is created, justifying the next binge. Friends, family, and others around the addict continue to try to connect emotionally with the addict's Self. They come up empty-handed, however, and at some point change the relationship with the addict to emotionally protect themselves. To have a relationship with a practicing addict is very painful and emotionally dangerous.

How Others React to the Addict

Friends and especially family want to make sense out of what is happening to the addicted person they deeply care about. In trying to understand, people around the addict label him or her in an effort to cope with the changes.

What is really being labeled is the presence of the Addict. The addicted person may get labeled as "irresponsible," "troubled," "tense," "crazy," "strange," or "weak." If people suspect the true source of the problem, addicts will be labeled more accurately to reflect what is happening, and how others perceive them. Family members use many labels when speaking about the addict:

- He's a bum.
- He eats too much.
- She's so irresponsible.
- All he does is buy, buy, buy!
- All she does is work, work, work!
- He does drink a little too much.
- He's oversexed.
- You just can't trust her anymore.

When the labeling process occurs, it's a sign that the illness has progressed to the point where family and friends have noticed it and must protect themselves from the addictive personality. People sense that the addict doesn't care about others. They will protect themselves by either removing themselves from or trying to control the addict.

Thus, for families, the labeling process is an attempt to control what is happening. Addicts react in turn to protect themselves. In doing so, the addictive defensive system becomes even better developed.

Becoming Dependent on the Addict

For the addictive process to continue, the addicted person must learn how to deflect the concern of others. One of the most dangerous aspects of the labeling process is that, once the addicted person is given a new label, the family starts to adjust to the "new person." This new person is given a significant place within the family, who adjust to this changed person and even become dependent on having him or her around. "The Addict" becomes a role within the family and starts to serve a vital purpose. Family members are caught in a dilemma: they hate the Addict but love the Self within the person. It's not typical for family members to realize they're dealing with an illness; as the addiction progresses within the family, everyone slowly adjusts to it.

Family members or others, such as co-workers, start to see what a good scapegoat a person suffering from addiction can be. They start to hate the Addict. As family members feel attacked, used, and abused by the Addict, they want to get even and fight back. Family members then become locked into the same fight that the Addict and the Self are locked into. The family tries to make the addict more responsible and respectful, but fails because a practicing addict is not able to change. The struggle continues, becoming a ritual embedded within the fabric of the family.

For example, suppose you love a family member who suffers from an addiction and is unable to love you back. You have deep mood swings, as the person you love swings from the Self to the Addict. One minute you may be relating quite well to the person's Self; then something is said that awakens the Addict. The personality shift occurs, and the next minute you are hating the person, trying to figure out what happened. Perhaps you made a caring statement that triggered feelings of shame in the person and out came the Addict to protect his or her territory

Because the person suffering from the addiction acts untrustworthy, the family stops trusting the person, and the members consciously or unconsciously start to distance themselves. This is a natural means of protection. When the person starts to act like his or her Self again, not like the Addict, family members start to feel ashamed for having distanced themselves. They decide to reach out once more, only to feel betrayed once again. This goes on and on until a family member cannot take it anymore and gives up trying to have any relationship with the person. But whenever family members feel the person's Self trying to emerge, they will feel a longing to connect, but also a sense of shame for not wanting to for fear they will be hurt once again.

Increasing the Addictive Process

In the negative label that gets attached during the addictive process, an addictive personality finds more freedom to act irresponsibly. Addicts themselves buy into these negative labels, and this adds much shame to their lives. The labeling process is frightening for both the addict and the family involved, for it is a way of acknowledging the danger they live with daily. The labeling process is but one change that is happening to the addict and to people surrounding the addict.

It is through this dishonest interaction with others that the delusion system of the addict becomes complete. In Stage Two, an addict's delusion system and defense system are used repeatedly and are increasingly relied upon. The addict begins to feel more confidence in the ability to manipulate others, but the addict's Self feels more shameful, lost, and isolated. Addicts feel like strangers within themselves. No one knows better than those who suffer from addiction the pain, anger, and despair of being emotionally and spiritually cut off from others and from themselves. This continued discomfort of emotional and spiritual desperation causes the Self to reach to the Addict for relief, sinking deeper into the addiction.

Pain and anger fuel the addictive process and are major by-products of addiction, both for addicts and those who surround them. As pain or stress increases, the addict feels more justified in acting out. Because of this, and because addicts adjust to the mood change produced by their acting out over time, they feel a need to act out more frequently and with greater intensity.

Being Out of Control

Addicts develop what is called a "tolerance," which simply means they get used to the mood change produced by their acting out. The mood change that once provided a high isn't enough anymore. Because of this tolerance and the increased anger and pain levels, addicts in Stage Two start to act out more frequently and in more dangerous ways.

Episodes such as these are very frightening for addicts because something they have felt inside for a long time is confirmed: they are out of control. These episodes are often followed by a flurry of promises to stop acting out and start "acting right." Addicts make such promises to convince themselves that they are in control or at least will be in the future.

The addict reaches deep inside, gathers all remaining willpower, and "acts right" for as long as possible. But as soon as the fear or shame wears off or gets pushed deep enough inside, the Addict regains full control over the Self, and the person returns to acting out.

At times, acting out can be a way of dealing with the shame. After intense episodes of acting out, the addict needs to make sense out of what happened and turns to his or her delusion system and addictive logic for an answer. Using addictive logic, the person finds a way to explain away what is happening, protecting the addictive personality and the acting-out behavior.

A compulsive gambler might believe her financial trouble isn't due to gambling, but rather because she had a bad tip or her house payment is too big. The shoplifter believes his problems stem from his family and his troubled emotions, not from stealing.

Because of the delusion system, it is nearly impossible for addicts to see the true reasons they are hurting. They believe it's because people don't understand them or because the world is a tough place to live.

Energy Drain

Part of the attractiveness of an addictive lifestyle is believing one has control over one's world. Ironically, it is the addict's search for control that causes him or her to have less of it. In a world of objects and events, the addict's increased search for control, increased loss of control, and increased shame all lead to more emotional isolation and produce tremendous emotional and psychological stress.

To live this addictive lifestyle, addicts in Stage Two must rechannel their energies. More energy is redirected to the addictive process. Activities and people who were important in the past are now less important. The person suffering from addiction finds it difficult to live two lives. Thus, something has to go. Time with family, old friends, and hobbies is set aside to make room for the addiction. Energy once directed toward others and the Self in caring ways is now used to sustain an addictive relationship. Addiction will continuously demand more, and because the addicted person has lost control, he or she must give in to the demand.

Once again, there is an almost constant battle between Self and Addict. *Should I act out or shouldn't I act out? . . . It's okay to act out! . . . It's not okay to act out! . . . I'll get in trouble! . . . I don't care if I get in trouble!* Many people in recovery report having acted out simply to be done with this internal battle if only for a brief period of time. This struggle for control requires an enormous amount of energy. Like any other progressive illness, addiction will take more of a person's energy, focus, and ability to function, eroding the ability to be a "normal" human being.

Spiritual Emptiness

As the addictive personality gains more control and addicts lose more of their ability to influence their own thoughts and behavior, a spiritual deadening takes place. Here the definition of *spiritual* involves being connected in a meaningful way to the world. It involves having the ability to extract meaning from one's experiences. The feeling of belonging and being an important part of the world is lost as addiction progresses. The sense of knowing oneself and one's value drifts farther and farther away.

Addiction is a spiritual disease. Everybody has the ability to connect with the soul and spirit of others. Because addiction is a direct assault against the Self, it is also a direct attack on the spirit or soul of the person suffering from an addiction. A person's spirit sustains life; addiction leads to spiritual death.

The longer the addiction goes on, the more spiritually isolated the person becomes. This is the saddest and most frightening aspect of addiction. Sunsets, smiles, laughter, support from others, and other things that nourish the spirit come to mean less as acting out becomes more important. Because addiction blocks a person's ability to effectively connect with his or her own spirit, there is little chance to connect with the spirit of others. Relationships with others become more superficial as the illness progresses. Addicts stay isolated or turn to the presence of other addicts who offer companionship and little or no fear of confrontation.

As addiction progresses, spiritual deadening deepens. This may be the most dangerous aspect of addiction. For recovery to begin, there must be a recommitment to the nurturing of one's spirit. The farther one moves away from the Self, the harder it is to reestablish a healing relationship. In the beginning of the addictive process, the person grasped the addiction in an attempt to nurture life, spirit, and the Self in the process of chasing perfection. Many recovering addicts firmly grasp the spiritual aspect of recovery because most are extremely grateful to have such a precious gift returned: the Self, a spiritual awareness, and the ability to connect with others in a meaningful, nurturing way.

Stage Three: Life Breakdown

Stage Three occurs because addiction works so well at producing pain, fear, shame, loneliness, and anger. Addiction creates these feelings in order for the Addict to gain control over the Self. It creates the need for relief, promising that relief will be found in the mood change.

By Stage Three, the addictive personality is in total control. The Addict doesn't care what happens to others, nor does it care what happens to the person who suffers from addiction. What it cares about is achieving and maintaining total control over the person and his or her environment. What it cares about is getting high from acting out.

Stage Three is named the Life Breakdown Stage because here the addicted person's life will literally start to break down under the tremendous stress caused by ever-increasing pain, anger, and fear that results from continuously acting out. There is a point where a person emotionally, mentally, spiritually, and, finally, physically breaks down under the stress and pain produced by the addiction.

Acting Out Breaks Down

By Stage Three, acting out no longer produces much pleasure. Preoccupation and acting out still produce a mood change, but by now there is too much pain to escape from. Although the addicted person feels more distance from pain while acting out, the pain's presence is now almost always felt.

The magical aspect of addiction—the intoxication, the high—begins to break down under stress because the person is living on emotional overload. Acting out can start to feel more boring and ritualized. Many recovering addicts report that at this stage their preoccupation with acting out and dwelling in a fantasy world produced as much or more pleasure and relief as actually acting out did.

By Stage Three, addicts start behaving in ways they never thought possible. The behavior is so extreme that it scares the addict. In this stage the dangerous life-threatening aspects of the addictive process become obvious, not only to the addict, but also to family and friends. At this stage, the addict is totally committed to the addictive process and will not be able to break this cycle without some form of intervention.

Addictive Logic Breaks Down

In Stage Three, addictive logic can also start to break down. The addict's behavior often doesn't even make sense to him or her anymore, so the addict gives up trying to make sense of it and falls into a lifestyle based entirely on addictive ritual. Thus, addicts cling to a very rigid lifestyle and feel discomfort with anything unfamiliar. Addiction is a very focused lifestyle and rigidity adds a level of comfort to the addict's life—there is a peace and security found in familiar rituals and objects, especially in times of stress. The addict may hate acting out, but finds security in it. It is something the addict is an expert at. Thus, in times of stress, he or she may quickly retreat to acting out.

New situations become nightmares for the addict. Life is totally controlled by the addictive belief system. Addictive logic becomes very simple at this stage: "get high and exist." At this stage, an addict will only deal with people and ideas that add to the addictive lifestyle; anything else is allowed to float by.

Coping Breaks Down

Resolving emotional issues works against the addictive process, which thrives on unresolved issues and the stress they produce. Unresolved feelings and issues are seen as excuses to act out at any time. The addicted person becomes an emotional pressure cooker whose safety valve is not functioning properly. Soon, something has to give. By Stage Three, the addict has so many unresolved feelings that he or she reaches a point of great emotional weakness. Existing coping skills do not provide enough safety to deal with the pressures that are being created. Emotionally, the person starts to break down.

The person may cry uncontrollably for the slightest reason. One recovering addict said that, in this stage, she had cried uncontrollably whenever she saw a sunrise. She later realized that this was because she dreaded the thought of having to spend one more day living the life of an addict.

At this point in the addictive process, people also may go into fits of rage for no apparent reason. Their anger has piled up and been compacted to the point at which it isn't anger anymore, but rage.

Paranoia results as the addict starts to question everyone and everything. "Why?" becomes a torturous question that's constantly asked internally. This can transform into free-floating anxiety, which strikes late-stage addicts and can last anywhere from a few moments to days. Those who experience this anxiety feel that the whole world has turned against them and that no one cares about or even likes them anymore. This aspect of the addiction illness can be very devastating for the addict.

Interacting Breaks Down

By now, the fact that an addict's primary emotional attachment is with an object or event, and not with people, has taken its toll. Many addicts start to feel less secure about interacting with people, even on a social level. People with addictions often start to question their ability to be around others. They start to feel as if people can see right through them.

An addict interacts with others by manipulating and using them to fulfill addictive needs. Doing this takes a certain amount of self-confidence and an ability to assert oneself or an ability to appear helpless to get others to act as caretakers. In Stage Three, addicts start to feel very unsure of themselves and often start to lose some of their ability to manipulate. They find people to care for them, but these people often do this out of pity or obligation, not manipulation. Many of those around the addict recognize the addict's style of manipulation and react less to it or get fed up with it and withdraw. They often have much of their own pain from interacting with the addict and make an emotional decision not to believe in the person anymore. In order to protect their feelings, they refuse to see the addict as a person anymore. For them, the Self is emotionally dead.

By Stage Three, addicts are often surrounded only by people who stay with them out of a feeling of responsibility or pity, or who feel too guilty to leave, or who are afraid the addict will become seriously hurt if they leave. This becomes emotional blackmail, as addicts often try to promote these feelings in others to get them to stay.

The Addict: Wanting to Be Alone

In this late stage of addiction, addicts may totally withdraw from others. After all, the addict's ritual of acting out is most often a solitary act done with no one around or done only in the presence of other addicts:

- Compulsive eaters most often binge in private.
- The gambling process is a private, internal strategy.
- Shoplifting is a private act.
- Sex addicts retreat into a private world often filled only by other sex addicts, if by anyone else at all.

It's natural that as the addictive personality develops and gains more control in a person's life, skills used to maintain personal relationships will start to weaken.

By Stage Three there is little in the person's life that is permanent and doesn't pertain to the addiction. The person has become totally afraid of intimacy and stays away from any sign of it. Addicts frequently believe others are the cause of their problems. They think people can't understand them. Thus, people are to be avoided.

The Self: Not Wanting to Be Alone

Deep inside the addicted person, the aloneness and isolation create a center that is craving emotional connection with others. Addicts are afraid of ending up alone. In their desperation, they show a childlike quality: they attempt to connect with others by clinging to family or friends and often become very upset if it appears that people are withdrawing from them. When a loved one leaves the house, for example, the addict has to know where that person is going. The addict will probably ask, "When will you be back?" and, "Do you really have to go?" The addicted person's Self clings to family and friends in this emotionally dependent style.

Addicts behave as if they are telling people to stay away, but when people do withdraw, addicts become quite upset. Loved ones hear the following from the addict:

- You can't leave me, you're all I have!
- Please, please, I'm sorry, I promise I'll do better.
- Oh, just one more chance, I promise I'll straighten up.
- Okay then, leave! No one cares about me anyway.

Addicts may panic when family or friends show any anger or pain, even when it isn't related to them. *Is this the episode that will make them leave me?* the Self thinks. The Addict wants to be alone, but the Self is terribly afraid of being alone. Often at this stage, the only people in the addict's life are family members. This is all right with the Addict, for being with others has always been a burden.

Environmental Problems

Addicts keep testing the boundaries surrounding them. They may have problems with their jobs as addiction begins to interfere with more aspects of their lives. At this stage, addicts are so out of control behaviorally that they may get in trouble with the law. Breaking laws and seeing just how far one can go can increase the excitement of acting out. Addicts may also need money to support their addiction and turn to illegal activities in order to get it (this is especially true of compulsive gambling).

Thus, many addicts may run into financial problems. They spend large amounts of money to support their addiction, and the addiction begins to threaten their livelihoods:

- Americans spend 6.5 billion dollars a year on pornography and it might be accurate to say that a good percentage of this amount is spent by sex addicts.
- More than 50 percent of alcohol sold is bought by 10 percent of the people who buy liquor.

Addicts create problems with their environment because their acting out behaviors may far exceed the limits that the culture around them can accept:

- The alcoholic may be arrested for drinking and driving.
- The sex addict may be arrested for visiting prostitutes or asked to leave a job for unacceptable behavior.
- The shoplifter may be arrested.
- The food addict's family may demand that he seek counseling.

Physical Signs of Breaking Down

The addiction illness may progress to a point where an addicted person develops physical signs of breaking down. Addiction is very stress producing, and after years of such emotional and psychological stress, physical problems develop. In all forms of addiction, the person's emotional and psychological systems run on overload most of the time. Physical stress also affects the heart and every other organ in the body. Different addictions will, over time, affect addicts' bodies in different ways: alcohol damages the liver, induced vomiting damages the throat of the bulimic, and sexually transmitted diseases occur from sexual promiscuity. Addicts often don't take care of their bodies and see them as objects to be used and abused. It's impossible to calculate the total physical damage addiction does to addicts, families, and friends.

Thoughts of Suicide

In this stage of the addiction process a person may start to seriously consider, attempt, or even actually commit suicide. There are two reasons for this:

1. The internal pain is so great that the person wants it to stop, and the addictive promise of relief isn't working anymore. Addicts want the pain to stop, but they don't believe they can stop it. An addicted person doesn't believe in his or her Self anymore, and suicide starts to make sense, especially when using addictive logic.
2. Addicts become so ashamed of and hate the addictive side of themselves so much that they want to end the addictive relationship at all costs—to the point of performing a homicidal act against the Addict. No one hates the Addict more than the person suffering from the addiction.

Stuck in Stage Three

Addicts can't break the addictive process alone. Thus, they remain in Stage Three until there is some form of intervention, which is an attempt to break the addictive relationship. Those who try to break the addiction process find that addiction is all they know, and they return to the addictive lifestyle. To recover, addicts must learn a new lifestyle, slowly exchanging the addictive way of life for a new lifestyle including relationships with other people. These relationships add to personal satisfaction and allow growth.

The Addict's world is based on an inward flow. To recover, the person must learn how to reach outward and sustain this outward flow, which he or she cannot do alone. People with addictions are handicapped because they don't know how to reach outside of themselves, and will stay in an addictive relationship until there is some form of intervention.

There are many different forms of intervention. Some are successful, some are not. Like most relationships, addiction can be resumed even if arrested for long periods. People often end a relationship with another person only to establish an identical type of relationship with someone else, and the same can be true in relationships with objects or events. Yet, recovering addicts should keep in mind that addiction is not just a way of interacting with a specific object or event; it's a way of interacting with one's Self and the world. To recover, the person must not only break off the emotional dependency within, but also turn to the Self and others. In doing so, a person can discover a new way of life, which can be wonderful and exciting, though vulnerable to struggles and fear.

PART *3*

The Why of Recovery

Renewal

Stuck in Stage Three addiction, the addict's life is a downward spiral of hopelessness, despair, constant fear, and terrible loneliness. For the addict, there seems no escape from the pain and acting-out cycles. The addict is helpless and entirely addiction centered, focused on whatever it is—a drug, a pornographic picture, a drink, another bet, more food—that produces the trance, a momentary and illusionary feeling of well-being.

As we've seen, the practicing addict does *not* focus on the Self but perpetuates the fight between the Self and the Addict within. The two are always in conflict, struggling for supremacy, with the Addict invariably winning out. The process of recovery from addiction, however, is found in the renewal of the Self; in forming and focusing on a caring, meaningful relationship with the Self; and, eventually, in forming meaningful relationships with others and with spiritual principles. In an odd way, then, recovery is self-centered.

The process of renewal starts with truth, that most healing of all principles. As William Shakespeare said, "To thine own self be true." This adage, which is engraved on the medallions recovering addicts receive on the anniversary of their sobriety, is their bylaw. It sounds simple enough, but it takes a lifetime to accomplish, for the addict and for most of us. How is it possible? Where does renewal come from? Is it magic? No, the potential for recovery has been within us all along.

The Drive for Connection

For the addicted person, the recovery process can begin when the addict's delusional system cracks momentarily. The addict may see that he or she can go no further and may then seek help. In other cases, friends and family may intervene with their love and truth, which may open the way toward renewal for the addict.

Once the recovery process begins, addicts often wonder why they hurt so much. It is explained to them that, for years, their suffering triggered their addiction. Their anguish is all that is left of their identity now that their addictive careers are over. They begin to understand that unless they are willing to be honest about their condition and act upon it, they will continue to suffer. At the same time, they must understand that their pain is the raw material that will help create their transformation.

To recover, the addict needs loving, helpful friends, an understanding family, and a suitable Twelve Step program. But the seed of renewal, as previously explained, resides within every suffering person, within all of us. It is a force that helps focus our attention away from our addictive impulses and toward renewal. Here this inner force is called the drive for connection. Placed vertically in the diagram on page 68, this drive is a constant, upward pressure that pushes us to seek out and connect with things outside ourselves and with something larger than ourselves. Erich Fromm, in his book *The Art of Loving*, describes this force as a desire to be reunited with the Divine. We may call it a Higher Power or Higher Principles. Within this desire is our awareness of being separated from the Divine. In other words, we seek a Higher Power because we feel estranged from it. We seek Higher Principles because we have a natural home for them inside of us. Our awareness of this separation often takes the form of guilt and anxiety, and this creates the force within us that drives us to connect.

Our drive for connection works in conjunction with two other drives we share with all other animals—the drive for power and the drive for pleasure. In addition, we human beings possess a fourth and most important drive—the drive for meaning. The practicing addict is a person who cannot create or sustain a meaning-full life because of the meaningless nature of addiction. Addicts unknowingly give up on meaning. They settle for living within and being controlled by their drives for power or pleasure. This is the Self wrestling eternally with the Addict.

Our view of life, what we value and hold as important, originates from how we order our drive for connection with power, pleasure, and meaning. If the major thrust of our lives is for power, we will define who we are by the amount of power we have. We will also work tirelessly to solve our struggles by force. On the other hand, if our drive in life is principally for pleasure, then we will define who we are by our ability to find, create, receive, and give pleasure. And if the major focus of our lives is for meaning and betterment, we will define who we are by our relationships with the principles of spirituality. While each of us is pushed by the drive for connection with power, pleasure, and meaning, each of us tends to latch on to one particular drive for guidance, comfort, and definition when we are confronted with one of life's many struggles.

The diagram on the next page shows our drives in the ascending order that promotes spiritual growth. As we are growing up, the positions of these drives may shift almost daily. The child's drive for power on the tennis court may switch to an intense desire for another ice-cold soda. If the soda is denied to her, she may discover that pleasure has certain limits or she may try to overpower her parent's objections. If this fails, she may discover the limits of her power, too, at least temporarily. While drinking a soda another time, this child might notice beads of sweat on the cold can and ask her

Pleasure, Power, Meaning, and Connection
NORMAL PERSON

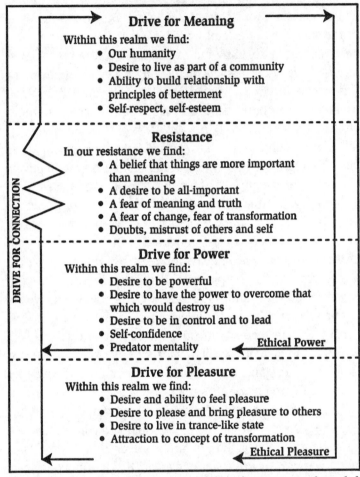

Drive for Meaning
Within this realm we find:
- Our humanity
- Desire to live as part of a community
- Ability to build relationship with principles of betterment
- Self-respect, self-esteem

Resistance
In our resistance we find:
- A belief that things are more important than meaning
- A desire to be all-important
- A fear of meaning and truth
- A fear of change, fear of transformation
- Doubts, mistrust of others and self

Drive for Power
Within this realm we find:
- Desire to be powerful
- Desire to have the power to overcome that which would destroy us
- Desire to be in control and to lead
- Self-confidence
- Predator mentality   Ethical Power

Drive for Pleasure
Within this realm we find:
- Desire and ability to feel pleasure
- Desire to please and bring pleasure to others
- Desire to live in trance-like state
- Attraction to concept of transformation
                                    Ethical Pleasure

DRIVE FOR CONNECTION

Energies from our drive for pleasure and drive for power get channeled through the practice of discipline into our drive for connection and thus create the energies needed to push through the resistance and develop our drive for meaning.

parent why this happens. The dialogue with her parent, in its way, is a search for meaning. Clearly, each shift of focus teaches the child something important about herself, about the limits of power and pleasure, and about the importance of looking outside herself for meaning and understanding.

Through the temporary loss of meaning and then its re-establishment, we learn about its importance in our lives. We also develop skills to work and live more meaningful lives. Ultimately, these shifts in the order of our drives can teach us about the infinite and eternal importance of our spirituality and the stabilizing effect of a life directed toward meaning. The pursuit of power alone, as we will see, leaves us fearful; the pursuit of pleasure alone leaves us grieving.

Unfortunately, many people vulnerable to addiction get stuck pursuing everything but meaning. They have the genetic coding and emotional setup to develop addictions. While they never fully surrender their need to seek meaning, they eventually live only for a fading sense of pleasure or power, as their addictive process moves toward the third stage. In effect, they short-circuit themselves, cutting off their drive for meaning by the pursuit of power or pleasure and always looking for the momentary, illusionary trance that will make them feel good and dampen their pain.

Before we explore the drive for meaning and its importance in our lives, let's first look at the two forces we share with animals. They, and we, could not exist without the drives for power or pleasure. They are essential life forces.

The Pleasure-Centered Person

The Pleasure of Pleasure

The drive for pleasure can be seen in its most basic form in the urge to satisfy the various hungers we have in common with animals: to drink; to eat; to procreate; to find shelter from the heat or cold, the rain or snow; to sleep. We share a need for pure pleasures also: we swim on a warm day; otters slide down a muddy riverbank; colts race each other across a meadow; swallows play catch with a feather. Most of these activities teach and prepare an animal for its future, but anyone who has watched a kitten at play has to admit that it must be just having fun.

For human beings, pleasure opens up many important doors. It is the first door through which we can sense the Divine. Through pleasure, we can transcend our present state and step outside the limits of space and time. Sipping a cup of espresso, chewing a piece of perfectly cooked tenderloin, kissing a beloved, or watching a sunset—all these pleasure-centered activities can be transcendent. For the moment, we forget our checkbook balance, the crime rate, or a recent airline crash. Pleasurable experiences give us a small taste of timelessness. We can sense what it would be like to step into the eternal, to be held suspended in a worry-free, peaceful domain.

But pleasurable sensations, despite their transcendent quality, do not last. Unfortunately, if we are pleasure-centered and have addictive personalities, we fail to realize that chasing and worshipping pleasure ultimately destroys our ability to create and experience pleasure. Our natural drive for pleasure must be surrendered. It must be combined with our drive for power and then rededicated to a drive for meaning. It is only by surrendering ourselves to the eternal that we *become* eternal. To paraphrase a holy book, it is only by losing ourselves that we can find ourselves again.

We can certainly lose ourselves in pleasure. People often do, repeatedly. But our drive for connection and meaning prevents us from finding complete satisfaction in raw pleasure alone. We always want something more and yearn for higher forms of pleasure. This craving, if it goes no further than the satiation of our instinctual needs, creates a pleasure-centered person.

Focused on Pleasure

When we focus our lives on pleasure, we measure life's values by the amount of pleasure we can get. We become seekers of two things. First, we seek the trance that raw pleasure brings. Second, we seek to avoid the anxieties and pains—what Shakespeare's Hamlet called the "slings and arrows"—of life. Avoidance quickly becomes the primary organizing strategy for how we deal with life. Struggling with life's difficulties becomes meaningless for the pleasure-centered individual unless the end product is more pleasure. Struggle itself is seen as a failure, a sign that we are inadequate, and this only intensifies our search for more pleasure. In his book *Love, Power and Justice,* Paul Tillich points out the dangers of this approach to living: "Only a perverted life follows . . . [Freud's] pain-pleasure principle." As we seek pleasure and live in a trance, we step outside everyday life and its realities. We become unskilled in the "how-tos" of creating a meaningful and joyous life.

Strangely, the more we pursue raw pleasure, the more afraid we become to let it go. This seems a contradiction. After all, that moment of pleasure can also be a moment of letting go, of apparent transcendence in which we merge with the eternal. What's important here is focus and context. If we are focused on getting pleasure and if our context is always liquor, drugs, gambling, or sex, then we can't let go. We're grasping, holding tight, and allowing our drive for sensation to direct us. All the while, we are seeking to control and intensify our sensations. The addict becomes trapped in this pleasure syndrome.

Pleasure stimulates primitive centers in our brains, which in turn can define and direct our worldview. This is an ego-driven view. Take the addictive gambler, for example. He goes to the casino, plays the slot machines, and falls into the trance. In the trance, he carefully monitors how he is feeling. If he doesn't win after a while, he notes that he's feeling bad, then later, even worse. He talks to himself about his rotten luck. Maybe he even talks to the machine. But it can't respond, unless there's a payoff. When there is a payoff, the gambler feels great. He's high. He can't lose. He's a terrific fellow. He's bound to win, even bigger next time.

Monitoring our own sensations is a personal activity, involving no principles of behavior. It only pulls us deeper into ourselves. From this involuted position, our egos grow and we find it difficult to form relationships outside ourselves, with others, and with a Higher Power and Higher Principles that keep our egos in check. Ultimately, pleasure-centered individuals value the objects that foster their trances more than truth, spiritual principles, or people. For the pleasure seeker, the question becomes, "How much pleasure can you (or it) give me?" Once a person or an object loses its capacity to provide that pleasure, or provide as much pleasure as it once did (an inevitable circumstance), then the object or person loses its value and is discarded for something that promises to be more pleasurable.

Pleasure-Centered Love

The pleasure-centered person usually seeks a specific trance he or she finds most stimulating. This section will focus on love, which might seem a harmless area in which to seek pleasure. Unfortunately, it is not.

When we operate in a pleasure-seeking mode, we often mistake the intensity of our sensations as an indication that they are somehow more real or, in the case of love, as "true love." We may also imagine that our sensory experience is spiritual. This is a dangerous gambit. We can easily lose our objectivity and sense of proportion and balance. Our sense of truth, our ethics, and our principles of behavior and morality may slip into a facile relativism.

As Americans we are infatuated with infatuation. Hollywood enshrines the notion that we all must be svelte and beautiful to be loved. Our advertising slogans broadcast a variety of notions about love that have little to do with reality: "If it feels good, do it." They appeal to our senses, to those primitive parts of our brains that demand action and instant gratification.

The pleasure-centered individual builds a system of values based on his or her sensations. When the focus of our experiences is love—being in love, making love—we soon find ourselves regularly falling in and out of love. After all, for the pleasure-centered person, intensity means we're really in love. Once the intensity fades, however, then the love must be gone.

The myth here is that the excitement of new love should continue at the same pitch throughout the relationship. Though we might wish it otherwise, it's simply not possible to maintain those early sensations. Neither is it feasible. The truth is, love varies tremendously in its intensity over the course of a long-standing relationship. Maintaining such a relationship often involves setting up boundaries—limits and definitions—for the good of all.

Such limits and definitions are of little interest to pleasure-centered people, who over time become totally tied to the impulsiveness of their sensations and emotions. This makes their lives and their relationships extremely volatile. As feelings evolve or fade, the pleasure-centered person is suddenly precipitated into a crisis. Not understanding the evolutionary nature of emotions, the person often declares his or her love moribund or dead. But authentic love realizes that joy is often pain transformed in the process of staying attached and committed to one's spiritual principles during painful and difficult times.

Pleasure-centered people, as described previously, are continuously monitoring themselves and their sensations. They may create the illusion that they are fully involved. They may marry, settle down, raise a family. But psychologically they are rarely fully *committed* to the relationship. They cannot separate from the Self because they are constantly monitoring their personal sensations, constantly seeking different avenues of pleasure. Thomas Merton, in his book *No Man Is an Island,* sums up the pitfalls of persistent pleasure seeking this way: "As long as pleasure is our end, we will be dishonest with ourselves and with those we love. We will not seek their good, but [only] our own pleasure." Authentic love requires times of self-sacrifice, both for the relationship and for others. It requires that people monitor the sensations and feelings and moods of others—not just those of themselves. As we will see, these are some of the fundamental lessons of recovery.

Intensity is one myth of pleasure-centered love. The pleasure seeker thinks that the greater the intensity, the greater the intimacy, the greater the love. This love myth is most sadly exemplified in abusive families, where intensity manifests itself as violence, which is then explained as a "proof" of love. "He hit me because he loves me," a battered wife says. Or an abusive husband explains, "I hit you, honey, because it was the only way I could get through to you." Or a parent tells a child, "I smacked you for your own good, dear." Intense though it may be, violence and intentional hurting are not part of loving.

Another love myth is the covert one we call "the good life." The good life comprises the right husband or wife, the right job and pay, the right house and car, the right clothes and friends, the right kids, the right beer and wine. But since this good life comes from the outside, we must seek it. To achieve the good life, the pleasure-centered person must act like the coyote or cougar that hunts, eats, sleeps, and then hunts again. The good life can never satisfy our hunger—there is always something new to be desired. Those who seek it are always on the prowl for newer, bigger, and better components of the good life. In this subtle way, addiction can turn individuals into practicing addicts and predators, and turns them away from their humanity. *They develop their skills at acquiring, sensing, using—but* not *in creating. They are beholden to things outside themselves for their happiness—whether it's just one more lottery ticket or a faster computer or a new lover.*

The End Result—Grief

This section has focused on those pleasure-centered individuals who seek to satisfy their cravings with pleasure and the intensity of its sensations. These people become predatory as the emotional and chemical changes of their addiction invade their psyches. While an addiction to sex may be more subtle than an addiction to gambling or heroin, it runs the same course, moving slowly and inexorably toward Stage Three addiction.

In recovery, the pleasure-centered person learns a simple truth: our emotions and the sensations we experience are not constants. Pleasure is *always* a temporary state.

A child discovers this at the beach as she tries to grasp sand that only runs through her hands or watches her sand castle succumb to the rising tide. As adults, however, we often forget childhood lessons and imagine that some of our pleasures can be experienced on a regular, almost permanent basis. Though the trance is momentary, we can seek it again and again, and maybe next time it will last even longer or be even stronger. But those who seek pleasure or power to the exclusion of spiritual values and meaning unknowingly seek misery. Even the most committed pleasure seekers discover that the trance always fades.

Grief is the major emotional by-product of a life dedicated to pleasure. If we are forever attached to something that is bound to fade away leaving us empty, we are bound to grieve, and, ultimately, to become bored and depressed. In this we are like Sisyphus, the king of Corinth, who betrayed the ancient gods. He was condemned to try forever to roll a huge stone uphill only to have it always roll back down.

Like Sisyphus, pleasure-centered people, searching the earth for sensations which always roll away from them, become attached to the world, to its things. Their souls become fastened to the earth instead of to the heavens. This causes them more grief, for the soul suffers when it is separated from the Divine. The soul feels ever more cut off from values, Self, others, and community as the search goes on for more intense forms of pleasure.

By focusing on one value, pleasure seekers close themselves off to the healing possibilities of meaning, principles, and values that help and enrich life. This only precipitates more grief, boredom, and depression.

In summary, personality traits of the pleasure-centered person include the following:

Vision: Life is painful, but pleasure makes life worth living.

Goal: To avoid the pain and anxiety that are part of life. To maximize one's pleasurable sensations.

Time: The focus is on the moment and controlling it to avoid pain and receive as much pleasure as possible.

Value: The value of an event, an object, or a person is determined by its ability to produce pleasurable feelings. Objects tend to become more important than people because they are more reliable and predictable in their ability to produce pleasurable feelings.

By-products: Grief, sadness, boredom, depression.

In the pleasure-centered person's life:

• Emotions are always temporary states.

- Relationships and situations are unstable because sensations are always in flux.
- One's lifestyle is reactive.
- Intensity is more important than intimacy.
- One's sense of happiness comes from a trance state, which is transitory.
- A positive sense of power is never internalized.
- The predatory side of one's nature dominates.
- The end-product is excessive, pointless hedonism.

The Power-Centered Person

Power: Right or Wrong

Like the drive for pleasure, the drive for power plays an important role in our lives. We could not live without it. The drive for power gets us moving and keeps us going. Beethoven used it to create his symphonies. A stallion uses it to win his place in the herd. From queen bees to lion kings, to the playground at the middle school, each animal and most of us use the drive for power on a daily basis. It is a tool for survival and for growth. It is only when it becomes our strict focus, when we seek power for power's sake, and when we become hooked on our need to control and be right, that we become addicted to objects, situations, or substances that make us feel powerful. We lose sight of the more important goal of channeling the energies of this drive into our drive for meaning.

People who search for pleasure have their counterpart and share addictive behaviors with those individuals who seek to acquire and accumulate power for power's sake. Power-centered people become seduced by the sensation of power and come to see power as a source of comfort and security. For this type of person, spiritual values and principles of life may be important, but they are not as important as power. Raw power as seen in the eyes of the power-centered person carries with it the right to define what is meaningful and what rules will be followed, as well as the right to gain more power, even at the expense of others.

When we gain power, we also gain a sense of self-confidence. This feels good, and we want to keep this feeling alive. When we are not in power, or not in control, we often feel bad, at loose ends, and vulnerable. We feel in danger and fearful. Feeling like this is an unbearable condition, and we immediately try to change it by gaining more power. We seek to gain control. For power-centered people, power in the form of control becomes the main goal. The more control they have, the more their self-confidence seems to grow.

Unfortunately, the self-confidence of the power-centered individual is most often illusionary. It contributes to the problem; it is not part of the solution. It is a self-confidence that does not build self-esteem. Self-confidence grows out of being comfortable around and using the skills of acquiring power. Self-esteem, for its part, develops through our ability to be comfortable and skillful at staying attached to and living with spiritual principles. It's the difference between learning how to play tennis because we want to show up our brother, and learning to play tennis because it's an intriguing and beautiful sport. Both self-confidence and self-esteem are components in the equation of power. They are normally relational in nature, demanding a balance between the two for emotional health. People who exhibit super self-confidence, at one extreme, or extremely low self-confidence, at the other, often suffer from low self-esteem.

Because power is all-important to power-centered people, they engage in behaviors that create intense sensations of power, which seem to build their self-confidence. However, this behavior also lowers their self-esteem. To maintain their power base, they will cheat, steal, lie, and engage in other neg-ative strategies that also destroy self-esteem. An example is a drug dealer who sells drugs to middle school kids and carries a gun. He feels high on power for several reasons: he's got a weapon, his symbol and sense of power; he's got a lot of money; his self-confidence is very high, but it's quite likely that his self-esteem is not; he knows what he's doing is dan-gerous and wrong.

Power-centered people struggle to wrest power away from others and to keep their own, and to add as much power as they can to their horde. Like pleasure seekers, power seekers work hard to feel good, and, for them, the best way to main-tain that feel-good feeling is by proving themselves "right" by whatever means possible. They may physically or verbally in-timidate or manipulate others to get their way, or they may argue forever to win their point. In the process, they will ap-pear to be utterly self-reliant, able to accomplish any task. They are irreplaceable, irreproachable. They often see them-selves as loners who have reached their position through their indomitable will. They think it's okay to reach their goals by resorting to secrecy and exclusivity, and to playing one group against another. Often they believe the end justifies the means—power at all costs.

Through all of these actions, power-centered people enter the trance, which gives them the illusionary feeling of well-being and safety from the chaos of not being in control. The trance is a comfort zone in which they are safe from fear and anxiety, but it needs continual reinforcement and replenish-ment. Thus, power-centered people are always involved in some type of power struggle, and the belief that they must win these struggles at any cost. Each discussion is a matter of right or wrong, and the power-centered person must convince the others, at all costs, that he or she is right. If not, the result is panic at the apparent loss of control.

The crack addict gets this feeling of power every time she lights up, and the trance produced is enormously addictive. The gambler gets that power boost when the slot machine gushes coins like a river in flood. He, too, is momentarily sitting on high, feeling very powerful. Within himself, the gambler begins a new round of arguments between his Self and his Addict. He's been lucky. He should go home now, tell his wife, and share the good fortune. But no, the Addict within tells him, he's on a streak, good luck is sitting on his shoulder, he'd be a fool to quit now. The Addict seems to be right.

The Power Syndrome

For the power-centered person, everything flows from the premise of being right, which gives the illusion of control and bolsters self-confidence (but not self-esteem). Being wrong is a sign of failure and weakness, and throws the individual into a vulnerable, fearful place. Being right invests power and righteousness in the individual. If these emotions are not counterbalanced by values and spiritual principles, they can become a self-fulfilling syndrome in which power-centered people insist they are right, and, being right, believe they have power, and having such power makes them right. This alternate building of righteousness and power is akin to the massing forces of hot and cold air that combine to form a tornado.

In the end, the power-centered person's need to be right—whether or not he or she is truly right—builds a false sense of self-confidence that inflates the ego. And the gaining of power and rightness, like the tornado's high winds, has a tendency to lead to destruction.

When someone challenges the dominance, the rightness, and the way of defining things, power-centered individuals become threatened and transformed into predators, seeking power and seeking to dominate. Thus, confrontation or difference of any kind scares them, unless they can control it. If not, they attack it. This is especially dangerous when a relationship is involved.

Like pleasure-centered people, addicts seeking power, or a trance that makes them feel powerful, are driven to avoid pain, anxiety, and fear. To protect themselves, they attempt to control situations, things, and people. This control, as already stated, is derived from being right.

The addictive gambler seeks money through her actions and in the seeking gets a sense or illusion of being powerful. She's in control, and believes she's going to win. If we win or earn lots of money or are lucky enough to inherit it, we can use it to give ourselves a sense of power.

Addicts who love the power trance use these objects and events that make them feel powerful to stay attached to the trance.

Power-Centered and in Love

For power-centered people, love is defined as an experience in which they lovingly dominate their partners or are lovingly submissive to them. This kind of love creates a dominant-submissive relationship, one that is actually based on dependency and enmeshment, not love. In this dominant and submissive "love" relationship, the dominating person is entirely dependent on the submissiveness of the partner, which gives the submissive partner a great deal of power over his or her dominator. Without this vital connection, the dominator loses his or her sense of identity. Someone must submit to feed the power seeker's ego and increase his or her sense of self and power. If the submitting person refuses to play this role, dominators may continue to pursue, harass, and stalk that person, searching for submission and a return of their identity and their love—their "fix." The power-centered person believes his or her feelings are true love, even though authentic love involves the surrendering of one's ego to spiritual principles. Authentic love requires ego deflation, which leads to ego transformation. It places principles before personality.

Unfortunately for couples (often addictive couples) engaged in this type of relationship, love is unstable. This is because any act of independence is automatically judged as a nonloving act and immediately creates a personal or relational crisis. Interactions are not judged by their quality but by their dominance/submission content. Whatever stability can be found in this kind of love comes from the clarity and acceptance of the roles each person plays. However, resistance and rebellion are inevitably percolating just below the surface. The submissive individual quietly chafes at having to do what the dominant person always says or wants; the dominant person is always somewhat irritated at the submissive partner for bending over backwards and being such a pushover. Both individuals fear any disruption or change in the relationship as they know it. They forbid growth and development and maturation.

The End Result—Fear

If the by-product of a pleasure-centered life is grief, then the by-product of a power-centered life is fear. Dedication to power produces a narcissistic and paranoid lifestyle that attempts to avoid anxiety and fear by maintaining and increasing its power base whenever possible.

If we center our lives around the accumulation of power, we will have trouble for a number of reasons: first, we must always test to see if our power can still make others submit; second, we must always guard against those who want to take away the power we have; third, we may join a group that boasts similar ideas. We may try to lead that group or become subservient to it and its ideals, allowing the group to act as a surrogate.

Addiction offers the sense and sensations of power. The amphetamine addict who's just shot up feels as if he's accessed all the knowledge of the universe. We need only glance at the history of the twentieth century to see what has happened to people and systems built on this kind of power, dominated by power-centered individuals and submitted to by power-centered followers. While these systems have all failed, or are failing, they have in the process destroyed millions of lives.

In summary, personality traits of the power-centered person include the following:

Vision: Life is a struggle to get as much power as possible; only power will bring true comfort and pleasure.

Goal: To get as much power as one can and push for what one believes is "right."

Time: The focus is on controlling the moment, accumulating enough power to make up for losses later, especially in old age.

Value: The value of an event, an object, or a person is defined by its power potential. Status symbols are important because they are thought to represent power.

By-products: Because power-centered people are always aware that they must hold on to whatever power they have or they will lose it, and there are always others who have more power than they do, they are in a constant narcissistic state of anxiety, paranoia, and fear.

In the power-centered person's life:
- Being in control and right is all-important.
- Relationships are dominant-submissive.
- One's lifestyle is narcissistic.
- Blame is essential, for to keep power, one cannot be wrong.

- Power is seen as producing pleasure.
- Relationships are important *if* they add to one's power.
- One's ego may inflate to unhealthy proportions.
- The destructive, predatory side of one's nature dominates.
- One's stability is tied to preserving power; despite surface calm, power-focused people are highly unstable.
- Whether one derives power from dominance or submission, the end result is the same—anxiety and fear.

The Meaning-Centered Person

Turn, Turn, Turn

Life is in flux. As a friend of mine says, "To live is to change. To live well is to change often." The pleasure seeker cannot hold on to the sensations of the trance produced by several shots of whiskey or heroin. The power-centered individual cannot control the next big win at the blackjack table or the concerns of his family whom he's silenced through intimidation. Through recovery, both someday may discover that life is a continuous process of resurrecting a new self from the one that preceded it. Both pleasure- and power-centered individuals thought on some level that they could avoid the daily round of anxiety, pain, and fear of the unexpected through participating in their addictions. As they focus their lives on meaning, becoming meaning-centered individuals as the recovery process demands, they will learn how to have faith in their principles and in the process of resurrection, rejuvenation, and resilience. Faith is the bridge that allows us to walk from the world of the seen into the world of the unseen, from the known to the unknown.

In recovery, addicts, whether power- or pleasure-centered, learn how to keep a proper perspective on life. Life, they discover, is a series of struggles and challenges embedded with

Pleasure, Power, Meaning, and Connection
PERSON SUFFERING WITH AN ADDICTION

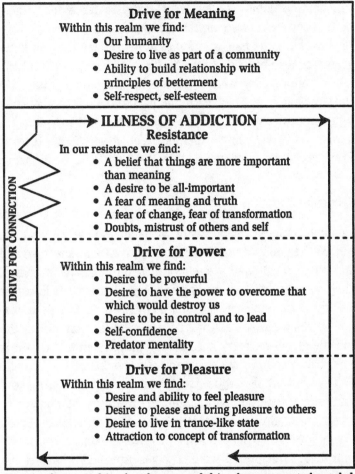

Drive for Meaning
Within this realm we find:
- Our humanity
- Desire to live as part of a community
- Ability to build relationship with principles of betterment
- Self-respect, self-esteem

ILLNESS OF ADDICTION
Resistance
In our resistance we find:
- A belief that things are more important than meaning
- A desire to be all-important
- A fear of meaning and truth
- A fear of change, fear of transformation
- Doubts, mistrust of others and self

Drive for Power
Within this realm we find:
- Desire to be powerful
- Desire to have the power to overcome that which would destroy us
- Desire to be in control and to lead
- Self-confidence
- Predator mentality

Drive for Pleasure
Within this realm we find:
- Desire and ability to feel pleasure
- Desire to please and bring pleasure to others
- Desire to live in trance-like state
- Attraction to concept of transformation

DRIVE FOR CONNECTION

Energies from our drive for pleasure and drive for power get channeled through the practice of discipline into our drive for connection and thus create the energies needed to push through the resistance and develop our drive for meaning. If the illness of addiction is present, the person, by engaging in meaningless acts of the addictive ritual, ends up with less and less meaning in his or her life, creating feelings of emptiness. The person becomes less and less skillful in connecting with and living from within the drive for meaning.

opportunities to extract meaning and ways of getting closer to spiritual truths. To live well, they learn, they have to dig hard and develop coping skills. Their struggles teach them these skills. They learn to accept the fact that life is a series of struggles involving the pain and joy of growth. They learn to move toward change instead of avoiding it or trying to protect themselves from it. They learn to accept that the future is uncertain and unpredictable. They learn that even though they may enter a program of recovery, their spouses may still leave and the Addict within will still whisper its sweet old song. They learn to embrace change knowing that their lives will never be the same.

Becoming Spiritual

Meaning-centered people want to better themselves and the world. They believe that it is better to give than to receive and that it is better to add to the world than to take away from it. They monitor their sense of personal entitlement, the idea that the world or someone—an organization, their family, a person—owes them something. They realize that the gift of life and the gift of recovery has been given to them and that it is now their responsibility to accept and use this gift.

This attitude demands that the recovering person make a continuous self-examination, taking inventory of himself or herself in relation to spiritual principles on an ongoing basis. Meaning-centered people work to develop conscious contact with these principles. Eventually, these spiritual principles become part of their being. In time, the spirit of these principles speaks directly to the meaning-centered person, in the form of a vital conscience. Vital conscience is the conscious contact of a Higher Power or Higher Principles. Finally, meaning-centered people know that to develop their spirit fully they must go out into the world. It is here they must exercise their spiritual principles. It is here they come alive.

Cast a Cold Eye

Meaning-centered people work hard to develop a healthy skepticism of themselves and of their own rightness. They are skeptical about their impulses and desires to consume. They continue to take a personal inventory of these impulses, working to control and channel them away from the addictive process and toward meaning. They work to simplify their lives so they are not distracted from what is truly meaningful. They accept that part of themselves is tied to the material world and wants to avoid the spiritual, but they realize that this is another form of self-indulgence, tied to power and feeding on self-importance.

At the same time, they are skeptical about seeing themselves and whatever group they're in as being right and all-knowing. They realize that an insistence on being right is a disguised desire for power, and they have a healthy respect for the seduction of power and self-righteousness. They know there are two ways to get power: by building and creating or by tearing down and destroying. They work hard to resist using destructive power because they know this form of power almost always destroys itself.

Meaning-centered people realize that there is a difference between force and ethical power. They know that force and violence bend the spirit of others to their will. Meaning-centered people recognize these instincts within themselves, but work not to use them. These instincts do not work to produce better relationships, and, more important, they violate higher spiritual principles. Ethical power, on the other hand, is regenerative. To maintain one's ethical power in a conflict, one must stick to one's spiritual principles. The recovering addict, for instance, may not want to report extra income at tax time, knowing he could get away with it. But he also knows that honesty is more important than money. The recovering person who gets up at 3 A.M. to do a Twelve Step call, when everything inside of her wants to stay in bed, makes the call because she knows how important it is.

The Moment and Eternity

Meaning-centered people do not try to control the moment but instead live in it. Through repeated practice, they strive for spiritual discipline so that they can stay attached to and operate from their spiritual principles for longer periods of time. The more successful they become at living in the moment, the more likely they are to live this way in the future. They understand that the moment contains their spiritual future.

By stepping into and living within the moment, we get some separation from and perspective on time. By living in the moment, we detach ourselves from the pressures of the future and its anxieties, and the past and its guilts. By loosening our grip on time and adhering closely to our spiritual principles (so closely that we become the essence of these principles), we transcend the confines of our egos—our desires and appetites— and partake of the eternal. We become the essence of God's principles. Our souls, not our egos, are enlarged. We are filled with humility because humility is the by-product of our transcendence. We realize the Higher Principles we will represent are far more important than we are.

How do we do this? We do it in groups by listening to others speak. We do it when we pray alone or together. We do it by taking the dog for a walk on a starry night and gazing at the sky in awe and wonder. We do it by stopping to take a long look at a tulip and reflecting on the beauty of nature; we do it by stepping into life—its struggles and its wonderment.

In summary, personality traits of meaning-centered people include the following:

Vision: Life is a series of struggles; by embracing these struggles, we learn to extract meaning from them.

Goal: To get as close to the essence and spirit of spiritual truths as possible. This can only be done by putting these principles into action. The ultimate goal is to be part of the creation of love.

Time: The main focus is on the moment and on putting spirituality into practice in the present.

Value: Principles are more important than the self. Our value as humans is that we can represent these principles on earth.

By-products: Peace, serenity, joy, plus the pain of constant change.

In the meaning-centered person's life:

- Little importance is invested in being right or wrong; spiritual truth is essential.
- The self is not seen as center of the universe.
- Despite life changes, one works to stay attached to the eternal.
- One feels comfortable, yet cautious, around power and pleasure.
- Power and pleasure are used creatively, not abusively.
- The ego is kept right-sized through humility.
- One works to love and channels energies into the struggle to extract meaning from life.
- One forms permanent relationships. Each person is seen as having a unique relationship with spiritual principles, and one can learn from every relationship, both negative and positive.

Spiritual discipline, then, is not an option but a necessity for the meaning-centered person.

Pleasure, Power, Meaning, and Connection
PERSON IN TWELVE STEP RECOVERY PROGRAM

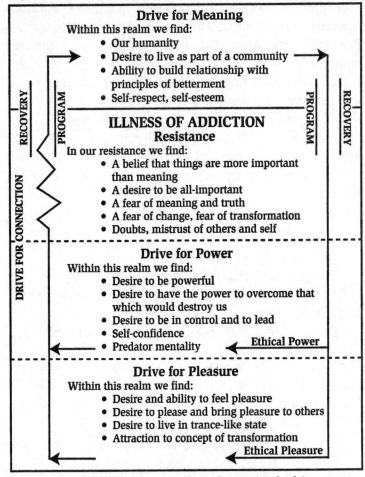

Drive for Meaning
Within this realm we find:
- Our humanity
- Desire to live as part of a community
- Ability to build relationship with principles of betterment
- Self-respect, self-esteem

ILLNESS OF ADDICTION
Resistance
In our resistance we find:
- A belief that things are more important than meaning
- A desire to be all-important
- A fear of meaning and truth
- A fear of change, fear of transformation
- Doubts, mistrust of others and self

Drive for Power
Within this realm we find:
- Desire to be powerful
- Desire to have the power to overcome that which would destroy us
- Desire to be in control and to lead
- Self-confidence
- Predator mentality   **Ethical Power**

Drive for Pleasure
Within this realm we find:
- Desire and ability to feel pleasure
- Desire to please and bring pleasure to others
- Desire to live in trance-like state
- Attraction to concept of transformation
                          Ethical Pleasure

RECOVERY   PROGRAM   PROGRAM   RECOVERY

DRIVE FOR CONNECTION

In recovery, individuals become more and more involved in a process and program that is fundamentally based upon spiritual principles of betterment. They are able to build a channel through the illness of addiction and reestablish a connection with their drive for meaning. The longer and more willing they are to turn themselves over to this process (putting principles before personality and practicing these principles in all affairs) the larger and more secure this channel will become.

Resistance

As shown in the Pleasure, Power, Meaning, and Connection diagrams on pages 68, 85, and 90, there is an area named resistance. It stands between our drives for pleasure and power and our drive for meaning. Our drive for connection which propels us upward toward meaning, can be subverted by our resistance. We can therefore stay caught in the cycles of power accruing power and pleasure seeking pleasure, and though we may catch glimpses of meaning, we will not partake in it in a meaningful and beneficial way.

Human beings have a desire for change and a desire for permanence. Though we have a natural desire to express our spiritual nature, we also have a natural resistance to change and to becoming spiritual beings. We resist the transformation of the self into spirit because it goes against our survival instincts. We fear we will cease to exist if any form of spiritual transformation takes place. Because we fear giving up our ego-hold on the things of this world, we tell ourselves subconsciously that it is better to stay in control, avoid pain through pleasure, and not surrender.

But if we refuse to surrender—to give up our attachments to power and pleasure—we cannot evolve and transform into our spiritual selves. If our resistance wins out, our drive for connection is redirected away from meaning and back into the drives for power or pleasure until we are able to overcome this resistance.

When we deceive ourselves in this way, we connect with others who are also deceiving themselves. We believe friendship and support come from people who agree with us and who mimic our views of the world. Regulars at a bar may appear chummy and comfortable, for instance, relieved from the pressures and burdens of seeking meaning and from surrendering. But if they continue to deceive themselves on a regular basis, they have begun the addictive process.

Getting to Meaning

The End of Endless Cycling

In Buddhism and Hinduism, the wheel of *samsara* refers to the eternal cycle of birth, suffering, death, and rebirth. Within that endless cycle are the smaller cycles that make up our lives. One of them is the addictive process—pain, acting out, momentary pleasure, more pain; or power, control, being right, feeling out of control, demanding more power. These addictive cycles are endless unless the addict seeks help. Once the addict surrenders to the need for help, the process of recovery and the renewal of the Self begins. The Self still struggles with the Addict, but now the Self begins to change its focus.

In the Beginning

The renewal process must start with honesty. The recovering addict honestly and respectfully admits the danger he or she is living with, in the endless drive for power or pleasure. Addicts must admit to and claim their addictive personalities:

- Hi, my name is Jane. I'm an alcoholic.
- Hi, my name is Bill, and I'm a sex addict.
- Hi, my name is Joe. I'm an addictive gambler.

Addicts introduce themselves at group support meetings in this way because this is who they truly are and because they want to be honest with themselves and others. By honestly admitting they are addicts, they can begin to have a healthier relationship with the Self, with the people in the support group, and with people outside of it. This is an essential piece of the recovery process. The addict learns that trust, which is based on honesty, is the basis of all healthy relationships. Without trust, relationships become struggles for power, rekindling the addictive cycle. Trust gives the addict time to heal and the freedom to connect first with himself or herself. Later, once the recovering addict has learned to trust and has gone through the steps of admitting and truly accepting the illness, he or she is ready to reach out to a Higher Power, Higher Principles, family, friends, and the community.

Forming a relationship with a spiritual Higher Power is an essential step for the recovering addict. In the early stages of recovery, addicts often find that dealing with people outside the support group is too frightening and shame-ridden. Through their addiction, addicts may have hurt both family and friends, and may fear their judgment and anger. A Higher Power, however, offers nothing but unrestricted love and care. By forming an intimate relationship with a power greater than themselves, addicts learn that their addiction was also a power greater than themselves. The addiction was based on dishonesty and destruction, whereas recovery is based on honesty and love.

Addicts also learn to slow down their addicted pace, which until they sought help was geared to high speed and focused, in the third stage, on nothing but getting more pleasure or power to improve a dwindling trance. In contrast, the healing process moves forward very slowly. Slowly, the recovering addict reaches out to a Higher Power and to members of the group. Day by day, sobriety begins to take hold. Slowly, one's dialogue with oneself begins to change its focus from the Addict within and from the negative and life-threatening principles of addiction: lying, cheating, hiding, accumulating, hoarding, and denying. As the recovering addict continues to attend group support meetings, he or she begins to have a relationship to the positive and life-improving principles and concepts of recovery. These principles eventually replace the addictive principles. Recovering addicts admit their powerlessness over their addiction; they come to believe in a power greater than themselves; they become willing to turn their will and lives over to the care of a Higher Power and Higher Principles· they examine themselves carefully and admit their wrongs; they ask their Higher Power to remove these shortcomings of character; they make a list of those people they have harmed and make amends to them wherever possible; they continue to examine themselves, pray, meditate, and seek out God's will; they awaken spiritually and carry the message of the program to others; and they use these principles in all their affairs.

As recovering addicts develop this new lifestyle, they work hard to be kind to themselves. They learn that punishing themselves for past wrongs and present imperfections is just another addictive behavior. They learn to approach themselves and others with the same dignity and respect they receive at their support meetings.

Self-Scrutiny and Vigilance

There are times in recovery when addicts feel and hear the subtle or not-so-subtle chatter of the Addict within themselves. The illness of addiction, as previously stated, is cunning, baffling, and powerful. The Addict does not simply give up. The Addict wants to be heard. Its arguments are clever and seductive. It causes self-doubt.

Throughout recovery, we need help from our sponsor and support group to monitor the Addict within. The Addict will look for other people, objects, or events with which to form a power-centered or pleasure-centered relationship. The Addict within has a substance or event of choice—prostitutes, food, purgatives—but other forms of power or pleasure will do if the preferred addictive mode can't be had. For this reason, recovering addicts need to continuously examine why they chose a particular form of addiction. They also need to scrutinize how they are currently interacting with the world to see if they are doing so in addictive ways. They need to examine their addictive logic, beliefs, values, and rituals to see if they are following addictive patterns. By keeping track of their Addict and seeing how it works, people in recovery can counteract their addictive impulses.

The authors of the Big Book, *Alcoholics Anonymous*, understood this need for ongoing self-scrutiny of the addictive process: "We feel that the elimination of our drinking is but a beginning." They knew that recovery is not only about not acting out, it is also about redirecting the addictive process that develops, grows, and becomes full-blown because of the illness of addiction. If people don't claim and redirect their pleasure-centered or power-centered impulses, they may return to some form of acting out. They will find another substance or event that helps them achieve the trance. Or, they may become a "dry drunk"—they have stopped drinking but have not surrendered their addictive personalities. These unhappy people treat everyone the same way they did when they were drinking.

To recover from the illness of addiction, addicts must not only break off their relationship with addictive substances or events, they must also come to know the addictive process that takes place within them, and take the necessary steps to transform their addictive attitudes, beliefs, values, and behaviors. They learn to pay attention when they stop attending meetings, go less often, or find excuses for not going. When they replace slogans and principles with negative thinking, become secretive about their thoughts, feelings, and behaviors, and cut themselves off from the natural helping and healing process of their loving relationships, they realize they are acting in an addictive manner again.

Honesty and Recovery

Recovering addicts can stop the subtle slide back into addiction by dedicating their lives to achieving honesty. Honesty is what keeps recovery going. Recovering addicts may not always like honesty, but they learn to accept honest criticism and turn their weaknesses into strengths. They study and live transformation. Honesty toward oneself and others must also include understanding and compassion. Honesty takes place on the inside and its companion must be compassion. Honesty has nothing to do with blame or revenge, but everything to do with how one views the world.

Honesty, when allied with compassion, is about self-monitoring and sharing oneself with others. It is free of critical judgment. If one is trying to be honest, he or she will spend little if any time trying to figure out if others are being honest. If someone is generally a dishonest person, it will become apparent in time. Like honesty, dishonesty is a lifestyle, but it is at odds with reality. This causes discrepancies that eventually become obvious.

How honesty manifests itself changes as we change and grow. At one stage in our recovery, it may be very important to talk to our parents about our childhood experiences: how we felt, what we wish might have taken place. It might even be necessary to confront an alcoholic or a workaholic parent. Several years later, the truth of our parents' lives will have changed, and our understanding and expectations will have changed too. If or when we become parents ourselves, we will be able to see our own parents more clearly, in a more forgiving way perhaps, and another level of honesty will likely emerge.

Being honest, we learn, is hard work, especially in the early stages of recovery. It's like learning a new language. But the honesty we learn in recovery gives us a life we can be proud of, and helps us move away from the shame we felt when we were living an addictive life. In recovery, we learn that we have been the victims of our lies.

Relationships and Recovery

The beauty and joy of recovery is found in relationships. By forming healthy relationships, we overcome our illness. By using the word *we* in the Twelve Steps, we start to untie the unhealthy relationship between the Addict and Self and start to connect the Self with others, with something larger than ourselves. We break through the resistance that prevented our drive for connection from reaching out to others. It is through others—other recovering addicts, as well as other people—that we as recovering addicts develop the skills to feel comfortable with our lives and can experience joy, perhaps for the first time in our lives.

All people, except those who suffer from certain mental illnesses, crave relationships that comfort and nurture them, making them feel proud and important. Once we have established a healthy relationship, we need to work hard to create a feeling of safety and mutual respect within it.

Addicts are not adept at establishing healthy relationships. They are accustomed to using and abusing the fragility of relationships. Mutual respect has to be expressed in both words and actions: we must *act* in respectful ways toward others if we want to transform ourselves into respectable people. In this way, we each help each other get what we need and want out of life. Most important, we support others in our relationships by keeping them safe from our own insecurities and negative behavior.

Truthfully, we know, like all human beings we have meanness within us. We have lived it and expressed it, often hurting others in the process. In supportive relationships, even though we may feel like expressing ourselves in a mean way, we learn to choose, honor, and live the Higher Principles that promote good relationships. We recognize this is more valuable than any momentary sense of power or pleasure we might get from lashing out. We work at having healthy relationships instead of having power over another person. When healthy people disagree, they strive to settle issues fairly and come to mutual understanding, not to win out and make the other feel bad. In a healthy relationship, people know they cannot control others because this leads to, among other things, distance and resentment.

In healthy relationships, individual differences are seen as assets, not liabilities. Each person's strengths are respected and sought out when needed. In healthy relationships, there is no attempt to reshape the other person. We accept others as they are. Leadership within a healthy relationship changes hands comfortably, as different skills and abilities are required to solve various issues.

Defining Abstinence in Recovery

Recovery relies upon total abstinence from the abused object or event. It is easy to define total abstinence in addictions like gambling, drug, or alcohol abuse. It may seem much harder to define in addictions to food, sex, spending, or work.

Defining abstinence, then, consists of defining the addictive behaviors each individual uses in the process of acting out. Next, recovering addicts need to be totally honest with themselves and others when defining these behaviors. They will have to commit themselves to abstinence from those specific behaviors and rituals. Some addicts relapse because they define abstinence too loosely. A sex addict, for example, may tell himself that he can't visit prostitutes, but it's okay to view X-rated movies. Pornography, he will soon discover, can be just as addictive as visiting prostitutes. Some addicts, however, make their definitions of abstinence too rigid, as if to punish themselves. "I will never look at anyone as an object again." When they set up such unrealistic expectations, they often fail to stay sober in their program of recovery. They get angry and rebellious at the harsh restrictions.

We need to create a realistic abstinence contract to recover from those addictions that we cannot be completely separated from. Planning such a contract should be done with a counselor, sponsor, or someone who has been in the program for many years. A sponsor can help us decide exactly what substances or events lead to our addiction, and what behaviors would now be seductive enough to derail our recovery. With our sponsor's help, we can develop strategies to protect ourselves.

This is a dangerous time in recovery because we become preoccupied with our addictive rituals. In thinking about what it is that excites the Addict within us, we run the risk of re-entering the addictive process. That's why we need to work out a contract with a sponsor whose experience can help us through the dangerous spots. The alcoholic, for example, may have to decide that abstinence for her not only means not drinking, but also not going to bars, not traveling alone for extended periods of time, and not going to drinking parties. The compulsive eater may have to make a list of the exact foods he will eat at each meal.

Once we have defined an abstinence contract, we need to share this information with everyone we have chosen to help us stay abstinent. When we talk about our contract with our support group, the contract becomes more clear and real. Others can now help us be held accountable for our actions. During the first year, we need to reevaluate the contract regularly, adding any behaviors that may endanger recovery.

Guilt and Shame in Recovery

Addiction is in part about shame. Addicts feel shame because of their addiction and because of how they act out. Many people, therefore, enter recovery with a deep sense of shame. Others who enter recovery may not feel any shame at all, believing there is nothing wrong with what they've done. At some time during their recovery, however, these people enter a period of deep shamefulness as they look more honestly at their past actions.

In recovery, we work hard to unravel the knots of shame that have tied us to our addiction, kept us acting out, and perpetuated the addictive process. During recovery, we explore our feelings of shame to understand our addictive logic. We realize that as pleasure-centered people, we felt shame and depression about our addiction, and to cover the pain, we went on drinking. As power-centered people, we feared the loss of control that would come with admitting our powerlessness, and so we grasped for still more power and control by eating everything in the refrigerator or going back to the gaming table, certain our luck would change.

Recovery, we learn, is not about shame. Shame is a judgment we place on our own being, rather than against our actions. Recovery is about allowing us to feel guilt. As recovering people, we need to learn the difference between shame and guilt. Guilt means we have committed an action that was wrong or not helpful to others or to ourselves. We can then think about and correct the offending action, regaining our sense of self-respect. Though we're guilty, we can correct the mistake and be forgiven, and the mistake can be forgotten. (With shame, there is no forgiveness, and nothing is ever forgotten. Shaming families can maintain the same fight for years, undiminished and unchanged.)

Responsibility and Making Amends in Recovery

Responsibility is a cornerstone of recovery. We may feel guilty about the ways we've acted and about those we've hurt. This is part of recovery; it is part of having a conscience. But we must not label ourselves as bad people, for this can restart the addictive process. In recovery, we learn to change our perspective on ourselves. Our illness can't be cured, but it can be treated if we are willing to work on it. Members of our support group who have "been there" can help in the healing process as we walk through the minefield of our shame.

In recovery, we learn to monitor our actions, and when we act in negative ways we do not become shameful and defensive; instead, we admit our mistakes and make amends for them. Making amends does not just mean saying we're sorry. It means recognizing and thinking through our behavior: *Because of how I acted, there is an inequality in our relationship. Now I need to find out from you what is needed for the relationship to become equal again.*

For a person who, during his addiction, continually blew up at his spouse, making amends would not mean saying, "I'm sorry for blowing up at you." It would include admitting to his spouse what he has done, recounting a specific incident, and then saying, "I know this caused you great pain and frustration. What do you need from me to make up for this?" If her request is within his realistic limits, he would act to make restitution to her. By making amends, he commits himself to a change in his behavior.

By claiming responsibility for our actions, we may win back some of the relationships we lost through our addiction. We are all human and we all act foolishly from time to time, but shame is a distortion of reality that makes it impossible for us to make amends. In recovery, we learn how to see ourselves realistically, as human beings.

Rituals and Recovery

In recovery, rituals are as important to our renewal as they were to the addictive process, and we learn to develop positive, self-enriching rituals as a result. Instead of going down to the bar for a couple of beers with the gang as an addictive ritual, we go to a meeting to talk about the Twelve Steps. With other recovering people, we connect to the principles of recovery, to our own spiritual centers, to the spirit of others around us, and to a Higher Power. These positive rituals are about being connected, about filling our lives with meaning. They are about identification and commitment.

Many recovering addicts have a simple ritual: each morning or evening they read about recovery, then meditate on the reading. This personal ritual ties them to the recovery process. It allows them to recommit themselves to recovery on a daily basis.

Addiction is also about having few choices, because the addict is focused on the trance and the specific rituals leading up to it. Recovery, on the other hand, is about choices. The rituals of recovery teach us the behaviors that help us exercise our choices. By practicing these rituals, we bind ourselves to the new beliefs and values of the program. We focus on growth. We commit ourselves to caring and nurturing ourselves and others. Through our rituals and the symbolic language used in these rituals, we learn to develop and commit ourselves to a language and lifestyle of love, for ourselves and others.

As we develop our rituals, we learn to act according to the specific code of conduct of recovery. We treat ourselves and others in a respectful and nurturing way. We make amends for our past mistakes and continue to do so whenever necessary in the present. We take time to reflect and to visit and listen to others. We use prayer or other means to connect to our Higher Power on a regular basis, and we go out into the world and practice these spiritual principles in all our affairs.

The rituals of recovery bind us to the parts of our world from which we receive healing, nurturing, and love. Positive rituals are about faith and life. By engaging in them, recovering addicts connect themselves to others and start to have faith in people and themselves again. By turning to their rituals in times of trouble, recovering addicts can reduce their personal stress and, despite struggles, can seek opportunities for growth. They rely on these rituals to help them find meaning.

Recovery in the World

Many people come to depend, in a healthy way, on the community, the "we" of our recovery program. It is through the "we" of the group process that we feel confident that we can recover from our illness—not by ourselves, but within the recovering community. It makes a lot of sense that *we* is the first word in the First Step of any Twelve Step program. As recovering addicts, we become we centered instead of power centered or pleasure centered. We make decisions on how to act by asking ourselves whether or not we would feel good talking about it with our friends. We invest our energy in the group conscience and eventually develop a personal conscience and principles that work for us and others. In other words, we learn to have an interdependent relationship with our community. Ultimately, we see this as a worldwide community. We learn to be good citizens—first as citizens of the group, then as citizens of the larger community. We sense the "we" inside of ourselves and are glad to participate fully and joyfully in the world again.

How does it start? A recovering addict volunteers to come early to a Narcotics Anonymous meeting and make coffee for the group. He notices how good that feels. He remembers one of the slogans from the program: "You can't keep anything you don't give away." He remembers the stories of the founding members of Alcoholics Anonymous who, whenever they felt the urge to drink, would try to help other alcoholics in need. He learns that by helping others, he helps himself to be human.

It is written in the scriptures, "I give you life. I give you death. Choose life." This, finally, is what recovery from addiction is all about—choosing life.

PART 4

Family and Addiction

When asked, "Do families cause people to become addicts?" I answer that, while much research has been conducted and many findings revealed on this issue, we still do not have the final answer on this question. Concerning addiction to alcohol, Dr. Marc A. Schuckit, at the Department of Psychiatry, Veterans Affairs Medical Center, University of California, San Diego, writes: "Alcoholism or alcohol dependence . . . runs strongly in families. . . . A genetic contribution to this familial pattern for alcoholism is best supported [by various studies] . . . all of which demonstrate an increased risk for . . . alcohol-related problems in children of alcoholics."[1] Dr. Schuckit goes on to say that in some cases children who were adopted and raised without knowledge of the alcohol problems of their biological parents still had much higher rates of alcoholism.

While these facts suggest a genetic link, they do not yet provide scientific proof. Before that proof can be made, innumerable roadblocks must be removed. First and foremost, we need to work with an appropriate definition of alcoholism. In many current studies, alcoholism has been divided into alcohol abuse (harmful use, such as having an automobile accident under the influence) and alcohol dependence (chronic use). Tracing genetic factors for these two definitions is problematic at best because alcohol abuse does not necessarily develop into alcohol dependence.

Another obstacle occurs when we try to determine who in our families was an alcoholic two or three generations back.

Sixty or seventy years ago, definitions of the alcoholic were only just beginning to be clarified and most alcoholics denied they had a problem.

Still another barrier occurs when scientists try to pinpoint those specific genes that significantly increase one's risk of alcoholism. Is it one gene acting alone? Is it ten genes? Twenty? The study of twins with alcoholic parents does *not* show a 100 percent correlation. One twin may be alcoholic while the other is not. Or neither twin may be alcohol dependent. What does this say about the influence of genes?

Dr. Schuckit summarizes his findings this way: "[It] is difficult to identify specific genes directly linked to a predisposition toward a disorder. This is true even for relatively easily diagnosed neurologic conditions, where the mode of inheritance is clearly understood [as in Huntington's Chorea]."[2] And yet, Schuckit goes on to say, statistically the risk of alcoholism for children of alcoholics is approximately three- to fourfold higher than the risk for the general population, which translates to approximately 15 percent of the daughters and 33 percent of the sons of alcoholics.

So, while the role of genes is difficult to prove scientifically, statistically their role seems obvious. A recent study, reported in the March 1996 issue of *Archives of General Psychiatry*, offers additional statistics about genetic risk factors. This research showed that, depending on their genetic dispositions, men who at the age of twenty had to drink more alcohol than other people to feel its effect were at an increased risk of becoming alcoholics within the next ten years.

For this study, researchers chose 456 subjects and followed their drinking habits over a ten-year period. The men were selected so that about half had alcoholic fathers, and the other half did not. The sons of alcoholics who *had little reaction to alcohol* had a 60 percent chance of becoming alcoholics within the decade. The sons of alcoholics who *had "normal" reactions* had a 42 percent chance of becoming alcoholics. For the men whose fathers were not alcoholics, the risk factors dropped to 22 percent for those with little reaction to alcohol and 8.5 percent for those with normal reactions.

What does this mean? Once again, the *statistics* suggest that children of alcoholics are at a greater risk of becoming alcoholics themselves. And their tolerance level also is a risk factor. Greater tolerance to alcohol at the age of twenty seems to increase the risk of becoming an alcoholic within the next ten years.[3]

This new research and ongoing genetic studies help show us who is likely to be at risk. They help us understand that there are certain factors and family types that may push a person toward addiction. An analogy can be drawn here with the environment, its pollutants, and how these factors can make a person more susceptible to disease. If you live in an area with extremely high levels of pollutants in the air and you are vulnerable to respiratory problems (whether due to genetic predisposition or other reasons), you will then have a higher chance of developing respiratory disease. Your risk increases the longer you live within a polluted environment.

Families work the same way, offering certain polluted attitudes, values, beliefs, and behaviors that push members toward addiction or co-addiction. Depending on the levels of these polluted attitudes, values, beliefs, and behaviors, family members will have a greater or lesser likelihood of developing the illness we call addiction. Our society has attitudes, values, beliefs, and behaviors that are polluted as well that can definitely push a person with addictive tendencies toward addiction.

Here's another analogy: If both my parents have had cancer, my siblings and I have a higher chance of developing cancer as we grow older. It doesn't mean we'll get cancer, but we have a higher chance of this happening than someone who grew up in a family with no history of cancer. This is similar to people growing up in addictive families; they have a higher chance of developing an addiction. Is it genetic? Is it learned? Is it the environment? In all likelihood, it is a combination of all three factors.

In the next section, environmental influence on addiction will be closely examined. Certain types of families and factors found within families play a role in pushing their members toward forming addictive relationships with objects or events.

Having Parents Who Suffer Addictions

If you grew up in a family in which one parent was an addict, you have a certain likelihood of developing an addiction or becoming involved with an addict. If both your parents were addicts, your chances increase greatly.

Addictive families often produce children who end up on opposite ends of a continuum. For example, alcoholic parents will more likely have children who end up drinking abusively, or children who won't drink at all. The illness of addiction cuts into the family and causes people to separate from one another and develop different ways of coping with addiction. Some family members may become addicts; others will develop unhealthy ways of dealing with the addict based on the addictive logic they have been taught to use in the home. These people, sometimes referred to as "codependents" or "co-addicts," are prone to developing relationships with other addicts, thus perpetuating this type of unhealthy family system.

In both means of coping, family members become dependent on an illusion. Addicts depend on the illusion that they can escape the pain in their families through an object or event; other family members believe in the illusion that they can stop the pain if they can get an addict to stop acting out.

Each side eventually becomes dependent on the other. When children from these families begin their own families, they tend to find a counterpart: a co-addict marries an addict, or an addict marries a co-addict.

Thus, a generational cycle of addiction is formed. The family members have learned the language of addiction; when it's time to form relationships outside of the family, they seek out people who speak the same language. This selective search doesn't take place on a conscious level—it takes place on a much deeper emotional level. Often frustrated clients ask, "Why do I keep connecting up with addicts?" The answer is, "You speak the same language."

In our families, learning takes place as we watch and interact with other family members. Being raised in an addictive family, we watch and learn addictive beliefs and addictive logic firsthand. This is the language we are taught. If our parents are addicts, they will be teaching us addictive values and logic as we interact with them. Addicts teach addiction through their actions.

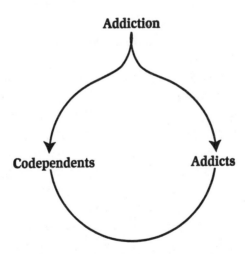

Addictive parents are constantly shifting positions within the family. One minute they may be all-loving, concerned parents, and the next minute they may act like irresponsible children. A child, especially a young child, in an addictive family changes along with the parent in an attempt to stay connected to the parent. Thus, one minute the child in an addictive family will be acting like a child, and the next minute the same child may be acting like a responsible parent. Growing up in an addictive system creates much psychic and emotional pain due to these major shifts and, unfortunately, teaches the child to adopt addictive logic in his or her own life and relations with others.

Emotional Instability

The emotional level within a family affected by addiction shifts daily. In the morning, everything may be normal, but by nightfall a cloud of despair fills the house. At other times, the addict may suffocate family members with love in an attempt to make up for horrible behavior the night before. This constant shifting and lack of stability either on a behavioral or an emotional level leaves family members feeling lost and unsure of themselves.

Children from addictive families often wonder where they stand in comparison with others outside of the family. They grow up not knowing how a "normal" family functions. They feel different from their friends and develop self-doubt, confusion, and a craving to know what is normal. It is this self-doubt, confusion, and lack of consistency that helps lead children of addicts to develop addictive relationships of their own. They may become addicted to different objects or events than their addictive parent in an attempt to avoid becoming like that parent. The child of an alcoholic, for example, may not drink but develop an eating disorder instead.

The inconsistency in an addictive family makes its members feel unsafe and unsure of themselves. Children especially feel unsure of themselves and unsure of the world around them because they don't know when the emotional winds may change and the love and caring of the moment will be replaced by put-downs and insults. This creates a sense of dread inside of them. Adults who come from addictive families speak of a sense of doom that always seems to be following them around. Ironically, this feeling gets worse when things are going well. They're sure something bad is going to happen. A person may believe a new relationship is about to fall apart, even when there is no evidence to support that. Another person may feel sure she is going to be fired at work even though she was promoted recently.

These feelings of doom come from living in a crisis-centered family, which is what addictive families are. A sense of doom comes from a time when doom was a reality. Good times in an addictive family are not to be trusted. They are followed by crises and personal danger on an emotional level. Family members are in danger until the addiction is dealt with and arrested.

Members of addictive families look for distractions or ways to become numb to the problems. They try to deaden themselves, and this is where they may start their own addictive journey. When Mom and Dad are fighting the same old fight about the debts caused by Dad's gambling, the child wishes he could stop them, but he can't. Instead he runs to the television set, turns it on, and tries to focus on a program. Or, he may run to his room and fantasize about being on his own, with lots of money, in a place where no one can hurt him. He's started to share his parents' behaviors. Like his parents, he is trying to numb his pain, or chase a fantasy in an attempt to stop the pain.

Along with these major inconsistencies, a person growing up in an addictive family is taught addictive logic. A young girl listens as family members explain away their behavior as if it were nothing. Inside, she feels crazy as she watches her parents destroy themselves. She tells herself this is crazy, but her other family members act as if what is happening is normal.

Inwardly and outwardly, people question the insane behaviors of the addict and other family members. They are met with what pass on the outside as reasonable answers, but in reality are total lies. When a child asks, "Why is Dad acting angry and yelling at us?" he is told, "Dad just had a bad day at work." The truth is, Daddy is drunk. When the child's friends say, "It must be hard for you when your father acts that way," he learns to pass their concern off, rationalizing and telling his friends that his father doesn't like his job, and if he'd get a different job, things would be normal.

Children in addictive families, like in most families, are taught not to betray the family by revealing family secrets. But in addictive families, family members are taught to lie—it's part of addiction.

In being taught to lie, family members are pitted against each other. The healthy part of them knows the family behavior is crazy, but as a sign of family membership and loyalty, they tell others and themselves that it's not so bad.

To survive in an addictive system, children learn to deny their healthy responses that tell them they are in danger; they have to keep increasing these dishonest coping skills because the insanity and the illness keep progressing inside them.

Growing Up in an Abusive Family

All children growing up in an addictive system are growing up in an abusive system. Addiction is a form of abuse because it handicaps children in their development. The needs of the addict come before the developmental needs of the child.

Abuse falls into two categories: *Intentional abuse* is caused when one person intentionally hurts another, whether the person regrets it later or not. Intentional abuse can be physical, verbal, emotional, or sexual. *Unintentional abuse* is the fallout from events such as growing up in an addictive family, losing a parent early in life, poverty, and other events that happen by chance. This section looks mostly at intentional abuse and how it pushes people toward forming addictive relationships.

If you grow up in a family where there is physical, emotional, verbal, or sexual abuse, you are being told that you don't count. Your needs are not important, but the needs of the abusing parent are. Your needs as a child—to be protected, to be loved and nurtured, to be treated as a human being—get pushed aside. The needs of the abusive parent always come first. You are being taught that you are just an object to be used to fulfill someone else's needs. In this way, you are taught the objectification process found in addiction. Addicts treat others as objects, and this is exactly what happens to the child in an abusive home, whether the abuse is being directed at the child or if the child witnesses the abuse. If you grow up in a family where one parent abuses the other, you are forced to watch people treating others as objects and not as humans. Your humanity is denied. You are taught that people are objects to be controlled and manipulated for one's own benefit. This will have a major impact on the development of self within you. Because you are being taught your self doesn't count, over time you will likely develop low self-esteem and low self-confidence.

You are also taught by example to have low impulse control. Addiction is an impulse-control disorder. As you watch your parents turn to hitting, yelling, or sexually abusing others to handle their emotional distress, you learn how to be undisciplined when it comes to your own emotional impulses. You are taught to be reactive; you learn not to take initiative but to wait for things to happen.

Growing up in an abusive family also teaches you to mistrust people. Abusive people are dangerous and can and do inflict great pain on others. We first develop trust within our families. But if we grow up in a family where our biggest danger is at home, where are we to develop trust? Parents have an obligation to give their children a safe home environment in which to grow. By watching their parents control or not control violent impulses, children are taught how to handle their own violent impulses. Parents have an obligation to be trustworthy and dependable for their children. If parents are abusive and untrustworthy, then whom are children to trust?

Whether to trust or not is a question that gets answered early in our lives, and is learned within our homes. It's part of the language we learn; it's part of the worldview we are given. When the time comes to leave our homes, we usually look for people who share the same worldview and who speak the same language.

Growing Up in a Neglectful Family

Neglect is a more subtle form of abuse. Individuals growing up in neglectful families often don't see themselves as being abused. Growing up in a neglectful family tends to leave people emotionally underdeveloped.

To develop as a child one needs input, interaction, and nurturing. In neglectful families, children don't get this. They take up space, but they're never sure if they're important. The self inside such people becomes underdeveloped. Their self-esteem does not develop to a healthy level. Thus, people leave neglectful homes more susceptible to the seductive element found in the addictive process. Powerful events, powerful people, and powerful objects seem to hold some truth to which others want to attach themselves; it is as if these people or objects can fill a void.

Many people who were raised in neglectful families have learned to be passive. They feel dead inside, and they will often seek out someone or something that makes them feel alive. They tend to see power in others or in objects, but not in themselves. One man with a gambling addiction grew up in a neglectful family. He explained that his addiction made him feel alive when he was acting out. He would put on colorful shirts and look flashy; he'd go to the races and feel alive and sure of himself. After acting out, however, he had to go back to what he called his "dull, empty world inside." It was almost as if his addiction allowed him a break from the passiveness he had learned from his family of origin.

Addiction is a relationship issue, and so is neglect. People growing up in a passive, neglectful family are more likely to be followers and to seek out people to tell them how to act. They seek out the life and excitement that was absent while growing up. The mood change they experience in their addiction produces a feeling of self-righteousness and excitement. People growing up in neglectful homes are very susceptible to this false sense of confidence and excitement. They get quite depressed once the acting out is over and their passiveness returns.

Shaming Families

A shaming family is one in which members can never do anything right or good enough:

- There are families in which a child comes home with five A's and a B+ on his report card, only to get a lecture about how he needs to try harder if he wants to get ahead.
- There are families with disapproving looks, "yes-buts," put-downs, and long days of total silence for not behaving properly.
- There are families with constant teasing that borders on emotional torture.
- There are families in which a child never feels safe.

Shaming families are families in which members are taught not to take responsibility; shaming families produce large numbers of addicts because they teach children the addictive process. Shaming families victimize their members in a routine, systematic way; thus, family members are taught to be either victims or victimizers.

Shaming families set their members up to be emotionally full of rage and to have, at the same time, a deep sense of sadness. Family members are taught not to be vulnerable, for vulnerability leaves them open for attack. Shaming families push their members to be perfect—perfect angels or perfect sinners. Shaming families teach their members not to be "caught" in the middle, for according to the attitudes of shaming families, that is like standing in the center of a room full of enemies—you can be attacked from all sides. Thus, family members back themselves against a wall and wait to be attacked.

Members of shaming families feel tension in their family system, which often is translated into a general mistrust of human beings. One woman who grew up in a very shame-based family states that the only reason she is alive now is because of the care and understanding shown to her by the only family member who would not shame her—the dog, who was the only family member she could talk with, cry with, and still be accepted by. In a family session with her siblings, she found out three of her four siblings had an identical relationship with the family dog.

Members of shaming families can develop a secret life, a secret side to themselves. This helps to push them toward the addictive process. All addicts have a general mistrust of people and have a secret side to themselves. Addicts are involved in behaviors they don't want to tell others about.

To shame someone is to abuse that person, but because it doesn't take the form of yelling, hitting, or sexually abusing the person, it is often seen as acceptable behavior. When family members are around people who come from nonshaming families, they often experience a sort of culture shock. When they act with what they think is normal behavior, others are appalled. Though we all have been shamed, shaming is not healthy—it is tearing someone else down to build oneself up. It is an attack on the person's self. The most dangerous part of this shaming ritual is that it is almost always done under the guise of being helpful or being honest. The person who puts others to shame will rarely take responsibility for the viciousness of the behavior. As in the first example in this section about the report card, the parents would most likely see themselves as trying to be helpful to their child. If their shaming behavior was pointed out to them, they might refuse to see their own meanness.

Children in shaming families often believe they are bad people and are responsible for their parents' unhappiness. To children, this is the biggest wrong they think they could commit. This becomes their biggest secret—*if people really knew me they wouldn't like me*—and they develop a lifestyle of proving they are bad people or keeping their shame a secret from everyone. As adults, they may feel crushed or become defensive if they do anything wrong or if anyone points out a mistake they've made. They are perfect candidates for addiction. They have the deep anger and pain for which relief is needed. They mistrust people and find a comfort in relationships with objects. They've learned not to take responsibility for any of their negative actions; if they did, it would mean, to them, that they were "bad" people. There is a wonderful book on the subject of how families and shame relate to the addiction process. I would highly recommend it to anyone who grew up in an addictive, shaming family. The book is titled *Facing Shame: Families in Recovery,* by Merle A. Fossum and Marilyn J. Mason.

Inconsistent Families

Growing up in a family where one or both parents act crazy is often like trying to play marbles on the deck of a rolling ship.

As rules, behaviors, and views of the world change on a day-to-day basis, there is nothing for the child to attach to and be nurtured by in order to develop. Children need consistency in their lives. In emotionally inconsistent families, the developing child is deprived of consistent relationships. In some of the other family types we have looked at, there is a consistent relationship, although it may be consistently bad and unhealthy. In the emotionally inconsistent family, a relationship of any depth is never allowed to form—all attempts are sabotaged. People who come from this type of family almost always feel unsure of their social and relationship skills and tend to be very dependent. It's as if they get locked into searching for the parents they never had. In this way, they are attracted to the consistency found in addiction. Addicts always know where their object is. They are drawn to the assured and confident feeling many addicts feel when acting out, especially in the early stages of the addictive process.

These people are also susceptible to peer pressure. If they end up in a group where being addicted to an object or event is the norm, they are likely to become addicted as well.

People raised in inconsistent families seem to have an extremely deep loneliness. They've been taught not to trust or count on other people. They crave contact and intimacy with other people, but they also mistrust them. As in some other family types, this influences members to have relationships with objects or events in which the illusion of fulfillment is to be found.

Inconsistent parents will often tell their children that their own behavior is normal and the rest of the world is crazy. The child is taught not to believe his or her own feelings or intuition. Children may sense that what is happening in the family is crazy, but their parents continually tell them nothing is wrong. In this way, they are forced to choose between their parents and themselves.

Young children especially will choose their parents' version of reality, for their survival depends on it. This helps them to overlook the inconsistencies found in addiction. One man came from a very inconsistent family, and found himself attracted to the consistency he found in his alcoholism. The periodic crises he had to put up with in alcoholism never worried him too much because they were much less frequent and never of the magnitude of those that were common in his family. He was never too frightened by his periodic blackouts, which didn't seem that severe when compared to his childhood when he frequently came home to find his mother trying to kill herself.

Death of a Family Member

Although the loss of a parent or other family member isn't part of the addictive process, it is a significant event that can have an impact on a person susceptible to addiction. While many times their families are very loving and nurturing, a loss this great can push people toward the addictive process.

Like addictive families, many of these families have developed a "no-talk rule" about the chronic illness or the deceased parent. It is as if the grieving process is not allowed to take place. Consequently, family members sometimes are not taught how to express or release their feelings of frustration and loss. Addiction seems to offer a form of release to them, as well as an effective way to numb their feelings.

Due to the burden that family members experience in these situations, they may live in a less positive emotional environment. Especially in families with a chronically ill member, much of the emotional resources of the family are used in dealing with the illness. In this way, it is similar to growing up in an addictive family. Addiction offers these people another way to cope.

Conclusion

Chances are you have picked up this book because you or someone you love suffers from an addiction, whether the object or behavior being abused is alcohol, food, gambling, or sex. The addictions from which people suffer are as different as the individuals are from each other, yet the common thread is a unique process that leads to the development of a distinct personality—the addictive personality. As wide-ranging as their addictions may be, the people affected by them can find an element of the Addict in themselves, and it is this side of their personality that leads them into despair and hopelessness.

Yet, this book has shown that addicted people can also share experiences of recovery. Through awareness of the addictive personality in themselves and by embracing recovery opportunities and spiritual development, addicted people can rediscover their lost Selves and live full lives of recovery and abstinence. In their search for meaning, they can overcome the illness that led to the development of the addictive personality and free themselves from the destructive compulsions that once controlled them.

Notes

1. Marc A. Schuckit, M.D., "A Clinical Model of Genetic Influences in Alcohol Dependence," *Journal of Studies on Alcohol*, 55 (January 1994): 5.
2. Marc A. Schuckit, M.D., "A Clinical Model of Genetic Influences in Alcohol Dependence," *Journal of Studies on Alcohol*, 55 (January 1994): 5. (Huntington's Chorea is a rare inherited disease of the central nervous system characterized by progressive dementia, abnormal posture, and involuntary movements.)
3. Paraphrased from an article by Susan Gilbert in the *New York Times*, 13 March 1996, c II (1).

Index

A

abstinence
  contracts for, 99
  defining, 98–99
  help from others, 99, 103
abuse
  as addiction, 112–14
  in families, 13, 74, 112–14, 116
  intentional, 112–13
  neglect, 114–15
  unintentional, 113
acting out
  breakdown of, 56–57
  examples of, 6
  illusion of control, 7, 8, 14, 32–33, 53
  increases in, 52
  and mood changes, 35, 52
  trance created by, 7, 16, 31
  See also behavior; rituals
addiction
  as abuse, 112–14
  acting out, 6–7
  admission of, 93, 95
  affects jobs, 60
  behavioral, 4
  breaking laws, 60
  causes for
    environment, 107–8

    genetics, 105–8
    learned behavior, 108, 109, 112–13
  co-addiction, 107–9
  defense system, 49–51
  definitions of, 1, 8, 10, 13, 23, 27
  delusion system, 35–36, 51–53, 66
  denial process, 30, 36, 38, 48
  dishonesty of, 15
  effect on relationships, 11–12
  emotional breakdown of, 57–58
  emotional logic, 8–9, 11, 17, 32
  financial problems, 60
  foundations of, 27
  fulfilling emotional needs, 13, 27
  and genetics, 69, 105–7
  highs, 3–5
  impulse-control disorder, 113
  intense experience, 15–17, 73–75
  intervention for, 56, 62–63, 66

people problems of, 47–48
producing a mood change,
  1–4, 7, 11–14, 17
producing a trance state, 2
recovering, 18, 26
state of intoxication, 2, 4, 56
suicide thoughts, 62
tolerance, 52
alcohol
  abstinence, 98–99
  addiction to, 2, 14
  arousal high, 3
  and elderly, 14
  mood changing quality, 17,
    20–21
  satiation high, 3
  withdrawal, 24
Alcoholics Anonymous (AA),
  6, 26, 104
Alcoholics Anonymous (the Big
  Book), 9, 95
alcoholism
  definition of, 105–6
  and genetics, 105–7
  in families, 105–7
  legal trouble, 61
  money spent on, 61
  mood change, 20–21
  physical damage, 61
  and rituals, 43, 45
amphetamines, 3, 83
anger
  addiction produces, 52, 55
  and breakdown, 57
arousal high, 3
Art of Loving, The (Fromm), 66
avoidance
  nurturing through, 7–8, 23
  of pain, 3–5, 31, 56, 66, 76

B
behavior
  addictive, 3, 4, 29, 95
    reactions to, 32, 48,
      49–51, 56
  changes in, 37
  dependency, 37
  learned, 108, 109, 112–13

C
change
  fear of, 68, 82, 85, 91
  necessity of, 84, 86, 89
  resistance to, 91
children
  abusive families, 112–14
  addictive families, 110–12
  inconsistent families, 118–19
  neglectful families, 114–15
cocaine, 3, 79–80
codependents, 107–9
community
  natural relationships with,
    23
  and rituals, 43–44
control
  illusion of, 7, 8, 14, 32–33,
    53
  impulse-control disorder,
    113
  in stage three, 55
  loss of, 29, 30–31, 39, 52–53
  and power-centered person,
    77–83, 100
*Craving for Ecstasy: The
  Consciousness & Chemistry of
  Escape* (Milkman,
  Sunderwirth), 3

G
Gamblers Anonymous, 6
gambling
  abstinence, 98
  addictive process, 15, 16
  arousal high, 3
  and delusion, 53
  illegal actions, 60
  mood change, 2, 8, 12,
    20–21, 115
  and rituals, 43
  satiation high, 3
  and trance state, 4
  withdrawal symptoms, 24
grief
  from pleasure-centered life,
    75–76
  process, 24

H
heroin, 3
Higher Power
  definition of, 22
  natural relationships with,
    22, 27, 93
  purpose of, 66, 72
  reconnection with, 66, 86,
    93–94
  and recovery, 102
Higher Principles, 66, 72, 86,
  88, 93–94, 98
highs, 3–5

I
intensity, 16–17, 73–75
intervention, 56, 62–63, 66
intimacy, 16–17
intoxication, 2, 4, 56
isolation

during breakdown, 59
emotional, 11–12, 23–24, 32,
  35, 39, 46, 53–54
spiritual, 54

L
labeling process, 49–51
life cycles, 1, 92
logic
  addictive, 33–37, 52
    breakdown of, 56–57
    in families, 108–9, 111–12
    and rituals, 42, 56–57
  emotional, 8–9, 11, 17, 32
  forming addictive
    relationships, 14
love
  authentic, 73–74, 82
  intensity of, 16, 73–74
  pleasure-centered, 72–75
  and power-centered person,
    81–82
  self, 29
Love, Power and Justice
  (Tillich), 71

M
marijuana, 3
Mason, Marilyn J., 117
meaning, drive for, 67–69, 85
meaning-centered person,
  84–90
Merton, Thomas, 74
Milkman, Harvey, 3
mood change
  acting out, 35, 52
  addicts produce, 1–4, 7,
    11–14, 17
  alcohol 17, 20–21